MARRIAGE MAKERS

MARRIAGE BREAKERS

COUNSELING FOR A STRONGER RELATIONSHIP

*William Rabior, ACSW,
and Jack Leipert, MSW*

LIGUORI
PUBLICATIONS

One Liguori Drive
Liguori, Missouri 63057-9999
(314) 464-2500

ISBN 0-89243-423-6
Library of Congress Catalog Card Number: 91-76662

Copyright © 1992, Liguori Publications
Printed in U.S.A.

Cover design by Chris Sharp

⬤⬤ CONTENTS

PART I
Marriage Breakers 5
  Introduction by Bill Rabior, ACSW 7
  Anger 9
  Poor Communication Skills 18
  Lack of Quality Time Together 27
  Stinkin' Thinkin' 35
  Lack of Shared Spiritual Values 46

PART II
Marriage Makers 57
  Introduction by Jack Leipert, MSW 59
  Exceptions and Miracles 61
  Good Ways to Fight 73
  Humor, Play, and Ritual 82
  Marriage and the Ten Commandments 91
  Marriage and the Beatitudes 99

Conclusion 108

PART I

⊗

MARRIAGE BREAKERS

⊙⊙ INTRODUCTION

I have waited a long time to write this book: twenty years to be exact. It represents the distillation of my twenty years of experience as a marriage counselor. Yet, it only begins to scratch the surface of what I would like to say about marriage.

For even longer than twenty years, I've been especially interested in the rebuilding, restoration, and healing of marriages damaged and impaired by the constellation of dynamics highlighted in this book.

I have written Part I of this book: "Marriage Breakers" (except for the chapter on stinkin' thinkin', which my coauthor wrote). My intentions are to pinpoint those ingredients that tend to grind away at the fabric of an intimate relationship. As you will see, however, these ingredients need not be fatal to a marriage. Each chapter concludes with a section titled Working Together. I offer specific guidelines that will help the two of you strengthen, maintain, and enrich your marriage as it is besieged by marriage breakers.

It was a genuine pleasure to collaborate with Jack Leipert, a colleague and fellow marriage counselor who shares my deep desire to minister to married couples and to assist in the enrichment of their relationships. May our efforts prove helpful to you and your marriage.

Bill Rahor

⊂⊃ ANGER

" **A** nyone can become angry. That's easy. To be angry with the right person, to the right degree, at the right time, for the right purpose, and in the right way is not easy."

Although those words sound as though they might have been written by some modern-day psychotherapist, they weren't. They were, in fact, written by Aristotle more than two thousand years ago. The antiquity of the phrase, however, does not diminish its powerful truth.

Anger is the most difficult emotion for any of us to manage. It tends to take over our lives, push us around, and lead us to say and do things that under normal circumstances we probably would find repugnant, even unthinkable.

Anger has a special power in marriage. Its impact is largely negative and often highly destructive. Having observed hundreds of couples who have sought marital therapy, I have concluded that unresolved anger between spouses is *the most potent* marriage breaker of all.

The Volcanic Force of Anger

Anger (which, in time, can shift to rage) eventually reaches the point where it can no longer be contained or restrained. When it finally explodes, often with volcanic force, the marriage may be damaged beyond repair.

Like human beings, marriages can become deathly ill. Too much anger for too long a time is like a life-threatening infection in the body. If it cannot be successfully treated, the "anger illness" may well prove fatal to the marital relationship. That happened to Karen and Ted's marriage.

"Ted and I were married for twenty-seven years before I filed for divorce," explains Karen. People were shocked beyond belief that I was leaving him, especially our five grown children.

"We appeared to be the ideal couple, living out the perfect marriage. We had a beautiful home, a wonderful social life, and great kids. Our friends used to refer to Ted and me as the Ozzie and Harriet of our community."

So why did this marriage fail?

Karen sighs sadly and continues: "People judge a marriage on the basis of what they see. But most of the time, that's only what a couple wants them to see. The dark side of a marriage is often hidden pretty well.

"The fact is that Ted was physically, emotionally, and verbally abusive to me. There were times when I called in sick at work and told my boss I had the flu, when actually I didn't want anyone to see the bruises on my face. And I can remember wearing long-sleeve blouses during some of the hottest days of summer to cover the welts on my arms.

"In the privacy of our home, Ted would fly off the handle at the slightest provocation and take his anger out on me. I was afraid of him, so for a long time, I buried my anger and hoped things would get better. But they didn't.

"After a while, I just couldn't take it anymore. My anger at Ted for his behavior and at myself for allowing him to abuse me was eating me alive. I actually developed bleeding ulcers. Our marriage became an empty shell with no life left in it. I finally had to leave to save myself."

Anger that has not been successfully eliminated from a relationship will manifest itself in a variety of negative and unhealthy ways. For example, the spouse who is unable to express anger, who bottles it up or "stuffs" it deep inside, may experience severe depression, a condition that eventually renders him or her dysfunctional and emotionally paralyzed.

Passive-aggressive behavior is another way unresolved anger can surface. Passive-aggressive behavior disguises or hides anger in passive and reserved behavior. This can take the form of procrastination, indifference, giving the other spouse the silent treatment, deliberately forgetting or neglecting things, and in general, finding ways to annoy one's spouse without letting the anger surface directly.

Unresolved anger does not simply vanish or go away. It remains beneath the surface of a relationship and becomes more toxic with time. That is, to say, it poisons the life of a marriage. As the poison is carried into the bloodstream of the marriage, every aspect of marital interaction is affected in some way.

Communication, for example, is damaged by unresolved anger. The couple find themselves distancing, avoiding each other, and no longer sharing even simple pieces of family information. A sense of basic compatibility is lost, and the couple feel estranged and alienated. Like a bad tooth, a dull, throbbing ache develops in one or both spouses, an ache that will not go away, an ache that constantly insists something is drastically wrong.

I am often asked why so many long-term marriages are ending in divorce. Although generalizations never capture the entire story, I believe that the primary factor responsible for the breakdown of these marriages is anger that has been ignored, repressed/suppressed, and left unprocessed for years, maybe decades.

Constructive Anger

Anger, of course, can be a perfectly normal and acceptable emotion. Spouses can — and should — be angry at each other when there are legitimate reasons. However, a little bit of anger goes a long way in a marriage — and most couples don't have a good sense for balance in this regard. The tendency is to overseason rather than underseason the relationship with anger's special spice — to the point that the relationship becomes unpalatable and lacks nourishment.

Expressing constructive anger is an art — an art that most couples have to learn. It is a marriage counselor's dream to teach a couple to process anger effectively, to put each issue of anger to rest once and for all, and to free their relationship of the corroding effects of unresolved anger. Developing such skills is possible.

Here is Laura and Jon's story.

"Our marriage was troubled for many years, but Jon and I couldn't seem to put our finger on the problem. All we knew was that we were living as married singles: two married persons sharing the same house but basically living the life of single persons. We had almost nothing in common. He did his thing, I did mine, and we intersected less and less.

"Eventually, I was smart enough to see a counselor who helped me discover that the underlying problem in our marriage was a lot of unresolved anger that went back to the early days of our relationship.

"I was angry because I got married young. I was pregnant and never had a chance to use my gifts by developing a career. Jon was angry because he felt trapped in a dead-end job and a dead-end marriage. Because of my own anger, I never affirmed or supported him. My anger fed his and his fed mine; we were making each other miserable almost all the time."

Did their marriage end?

Laura smiles. "Thank the good Lord, it didn't, but it easily could have. When we finally started to work on our relationship, we were teetering right on the edge. One more thing probably would have pushed us over."

How was this marriage salvaged?

"Jon went to counseling with me. He recognized and acknowledged his anger as well as our mutual anger, and together we started to do something about it. We had only four sessions with the marriage counselor: all the other work was done outside her office on our own.

"The work consisted of a lot of dialogue between us — plenty of good, old-fashioned talking to get our feelings out without annihilating each other. We really communicated, maybe for the first time in our marriage.

"The counseling was extremely helpful. The therapist suggested a technique that would help us facilitate better communication. Three times a week we would sit down together for a half-hour or more. I would talk for ten minutes. Jon would listen and then repeat back to me what he had heard me say, noncritically and without judging the content. Then I did the same thing with him. It was simple, yet it did the trick; it got us back in touch with each other's feelings. It taught us how to listen to each other without overreacting."

Laura pauses reflectively, then continues: "I have to be honest and say that today our marriage is by no means perfect. We still get angry and argue, but this happens less and less. When we do argue, we resolve things much quicker. We know that we really do want to stay married to each other, so that means we have to invest time and energy in our relationship to keep it healthy. With all my heart, I believe there is a hopeful future for our marriage — and it feels so good to be able to say that and mean it."

Although there is a legitimate place for anger in a marital relationship, the anger must be successfully managed or it will eventually come to manage the couple. If you're not the master of your anger, you will — sooner or later — become its slave.

WORKING TOGETHER

There is probably no single best way to handle anger in a marriage, but the following techniques for anger management have proven helpful to other couples.

Inventory your anger. Stop, look, and listen! Where is your anger coming from? How long have you felt this way? Is your anger totally unrelated to your spouse? That is, could you be projecting onto each other some amount of anger that is linked to other issues? Is your anger reasonable or unreasonable? Could you be magnifying or distorting things, blowing things out of proportion? Is this issue worth fighting over or is there another, less volatile way to deal with it? What will help the two of you reduce and resolve your feelings of anger?

Set limits on your anger. Don't let your anger get out of control. Under the right circumstances, it is all too easy for a tiny flame to become a roaring inferno. Don't go for each other's jugular vein. Marriage is not a gladiator sport, where you must win or die. Limit your anger to the issue at hand. Don't go back ten years and dig up things that will only add fuel to the fire. Make your focus as specific as possible and stick to it.

Don't turn your anger into a guerrilla warfare that lasts forever. Resolve the anger as rapidly as you can. Some marriage counselors suggest that fifteen minutes of arguing is enough. After that amount of time, give each other a "time-out" sign and take a break. If the issue absolutely has to be discussed, come back together in a half-hour and try again, but this time discuss, don't argue.

Draw on other methods to drain your anger. Vigorous physical workouts are effective anger busters. A brisk twenty-minute walk — together or separately — releases pent-up tension that otherwise might get dumped into the argument, causing painful damage. If there seems to be a recurring pattern to your anger, get yourself a punching bag and work out your anger on it.

Take a deep breath and exhale. Count to fifty — and count to fifty again — and again.

Stop feeding your anger with dark, hostile, negative thinking. Talk to yourself. Use self-talk to de-escalate your anger and bring it down to a more manageable level. Tell yourself to calm down and regain self-control. Ask yourself — and each other — if this anger episode is really worth it.

Separate your feelings from the facts. Having angry feelings toward each other does not necessarily mean you're dealing with reality. Has one or both of you misinterpreted things? Are you second-guessing or mind reading? Are you being petty or hypersensitive? Are you maintaining genuine respect for each other's needs and overall good?

Look for opportunities to compromise. No one is always right. If one of you consistently gives in to the other, feelings of power and victimization will develop; the anger will be trapped in this pattern. Compromising is a good way for both of you to win and come away reasonably satisfied. Compromising can be an effective way to reduce anger levels.

Listen, don't just react. Many spouses admit that they do far too much talking, that they do not listen well to their partner. They feel they have to protect their turf and defend their point of view to the bitter end. If this approach continues, the bitter end will come sooner than either expects.

Famous theologian Paul Tillich has said that the first duty of love is to listen. Listening is a major component of good communication and deepening intimacy. It brings down anger levels because it affirms the other spouse as a valuable person who has something worth saying. Listen and learn from each other. Listen and heal together.

Push for a rapid resolution. Ongoing quarrels severely batter and bruise a marriage, especially if the quarrels focus on the same issues. If you fight about the same issue again and again, you have evidently never resolved it; your relationship is bruised and in need of healing.

Try to resolve your anger as rapidly as you can. Saint Paul stressed the importance of not letting the sun go down on your anger. If it does, it will probably rise on your anger, too, and that is not healthy for either of you or your marriage.

Unresolved anger does not have to be the great unbeatable

foe that perpetually threatens a marital relationship. Anger can be successfully monitored and managed to become a tool for change and growth. But whether it becomes a toxin or a tool is up to the two of you. Use anger sparingly, carefully, and well. The overall health of your marriage depends on it.

Love is patient, love is kind. It is not jealous, [love] is not pompous, it is not inflated, it is not rude, it does not seek its own interests, it is not quick-tempered, it does not brood over injury, it does not rejoice over wrongdoing but rejoices with the truth. It bears all things, believes all things, hopes all things, endures all things.

1 Corinthians 13:4-7

○○ POOR
COMMUNICATION
SKILLS

If anger is the primary marriage breaker, a very close second is poor communication skills. In fact, the two are usually so closely intertwined as to be inseparable. Unresolved anger invariably leads to poor communication, and poor communication prevents the anger from being resolved.

A basic need for each of us, married or not, is to express ourselves, to self-disclose, to be known by someone else, to connect — none of which is possible in a healthy way without solid communication skills.

Communication is especially fundamental and indispensable in a marriage relationship. It fuels a marriage, keeps love moving to deeper and deeper levels, and reinforces the vital ingredients of trust, respect, and understanding. Good communication creates an environment and an attitude that says, "You can talk to me about anything, and I will listen to you and love you no matter what."

Consequently, when communication becomes impaired or ceases altogether, the life potential of the marriage is short-circuited. When this takes place, the damage may eventually become irreparable, and the very life of the relationship is in jeopardy.

I have observed in marital therapy that the breakdown of intimate communication is seldom an all-at-once event, followed by the end of the marriage. The erosion of communication usually occurs gradually and subtly. Without realizing what's happening, the couple slowly stops talking to each other. Finally, they distance so much that they find themselves virtual strangers to each other.

Here is part of Carl's story.

"Molly and I were married for almost twenty years. In the early years of marriage, communicating with each other was very important to both of us. We genuinely enjoyed talking to each other.

"We would go for leisurely walks in the evening or just sit on the beach for hours, holding hands and talking, talking, talking — about everything from world politics to the color we wanted to paint the kitchen.

"It seems like back then we had an inexhaustible supply of things to talk about and share with each other. As long as we felt that way, our marriage was extremely good; we were very close without suffocating each other. I guess you might say that our good communication during that time was like some kind of marital "super glue" that created a marriage bond we thought could survive anything."

Carl sighs and continues: "It probably would have survived

anything if only we hadn't started neglecting our marriage and taking things for granted."

What happened to the marriage?

"It fell apart as a result of neglect, not enough basic maintenance, much the way a house does when the owners don't look after it anymore. The children started to come along, and our lives took off like supersonic airplanes flying in different directions.

"I have to accept most of the blame for what happened though. Trying to make myself into a spectacular business success, I became a workaholic, spending far too much time carving out a career for myself so I could knock down the big bucks. After a while, I hardly saw Molly or the kids.

"We began to communicate in shorthand: quick I-love-you-have-a-good-day kisses at the door and notes on the refrigerator. Our sex remained okay, though, so I thought that as long as our sexual relationship was good, everything else must be good."

Was it?

Carl shakes his head sadly. "On our nineteenth wedding anniversary, Molly told me she was leaving me. There was nobody else; she said she was just tired of living with a stranger. She felt she could have a better life by herself. She said she had been trying to reach me for years to let me know our marriage was in serious trouble, but I kept ignoring her. I was shocked and begged her to stay. I told her I would change, but she felt I couldn't, and she left.

"Now I know she was right. Until I get my priorities straight and commit to really investing myself fully in a relationship, I won't be ready for remarriage."

Deep communication with each other can be as intimate an experience as sex, sometimes even more so. To share your innermost self with your spouse and to know that you will be accepted and understood for who and what you are without being judged or rejected is a profound experience of sacramental closeness.

Conversely, when this experience is thwarted or blocked, you naturally feel the pain of emptiness, and marital loneliness sets in.

Larry offers these remarks about marital loneliness.

"Loneliness in a marriage is something I know a lot about. In my first marriage, which ended after three years, it seemed like I was lonely all the time. I almost felt unmarried, as though I didn't have a partner. I felt isolated from the very person who was supposed to be my best friend in the whole world, the one I wanted to be closest to."

What causes marital loneliness?

Larry continues: "I know beyond a doubt that loneliness in marriage is caused by a basic lack of communication between two spouses. You can't build a friendship without communicating in a deep way. It just can't be done. Without decent communication, you're going to end up a million miles apart, and believe me, that makes for a pretty unhappy marriage."

In a healthy and dynamic marriage, the couple talks not at each other but to and with each other — not just occasionally when the mood strikes, but consistently. In fact, communication is so vital to a marriage that a couple courts tremendous risk when communication is stopped or is used as a means of manipulation and punishment (using silence as a means of punishing the other spouse, for example).

Amanda agrees.

"In my marriage to Louis, the silent treatment was my ultimate weapon. Instead of talking things through after a blowup, or sometimes even a minor disagreement, I would clam up — sometimes for days at a time. I ignored him; I simply pretended that he didn't exist."

Was it effective?

"You bet. I discovered there was no worse form of punishment. It devastated him. He didn't know what to do. I could really get to him, and we both knew it."

What happened in this marriage?

"After ten years of marriage, Louis left me for another woman. He told me that he wanted a more mature marriage partner, someone who was willing to dialogue about differences, not just retaliate. After he was gone for a while, I knew he'd been right.

"I've remarried, and things are going well. I force myself to be a communicator now; the silent treatment is a thing of the past. I learned my lesson the hard way, believe me. In marriage, if you don't talk, someone is going to walk."

The Art of Good Communication

The best kind of communication is honest, open, direct, and based on the desire to self-disclose. In turn, the other spouse feels an open invitation to share similarly. Through this deep mutual sharing, the couple continues to grow together because they are continually learning something new about each other. There is no chance for stagnation to creep in since the communication process keeps the marital relationship alive, dynamic, and interesting.

If communication is, indeed, an acquired art that is the lifeblood of a marriage, it follows that you should do everything within your power to enrich and enhance the ways you communicate. Exercising good communication skills helps develop the intimacy you share; good communication skills enable you to become greater and more passionate lovers through the years.

Good communication skills can be borne of poor communication patterns if enough work is invested in the process by both of you. No couple has perfect communication: perfection in a marriage is nonexistent. Nonetheless, if you really try, you can at least modify and change certain dysfunctional communication styles into ones that benefit your marriage.

Dan and Ellen did just that.

"Dan and I really did feel that we were stagnated in the ways we related to each other, so we decided to do something about it. Our local community college offered a communication skills course for couples, so we went to it together.

"We also made a Marriage Encounter, which stressed the importance of deep communication. I can't tell you how much our marriage improved. Now we communicate more in some ways and less in others, but the overall effect has been extremely positive for our marriage."

⊘ WORKING TOGETHER

The following tips for improving marital communication have proven helpful for many couples I've worked with over the years.

Make and take time to communicate. You need to prioritize communicating with each other so that it actually does take place. That means making and taking time to talk.

Where do you do your best talking? in your bedroom? on the couch? in the car? at the breakfast table? Identify the place where you talk the best with each other, then maximize the time in that location.

Make communication happen — or it may not.

Agree to disagree at times. Communication is not meant to create competition. Its purpose is to lead toward understanding and acceptance — not toward control and a victory of some sort. Nor does communication mean uniformity in thinking; you do not have to agree with each other all the time.

It's perfectly fine to disagree. Disagreements occur in even the healthiest, most alive marriages. Because you are not clones of each other, you should and will disagree as an expression of your individuality.

Bear in mind, however, that your right to disagree does not mean you have the right to damage each other. When it comes to this aspect of communication, the essential ingredient has to be respect. If you genuinely respect each other, you'll continue to communicate, even when you strongly disagree. Your relationship will remain intact and even improve by the healthy interaction. Disagree all you want, but in the process, *do not* hurt each other.

Diversify communication patterns. Communication is much more than just talking. It is multifaceted and may take on different forms in different situations.

For example, there are many nonverbal ways to communicate deeply without saying a word. In many situations, eye contact, a hug, an embrace, or a kiss will say much more than words. Body language is a language in itself and can speak volumes.

In marriage counseling, I frequently notice that couples who are having difficulty communicating verbally also have difficulty touching. Sometimes communication patterns that have been damaged can actually be healed by gentle touching, as the spouses rediscover unity through touch.

Another effective way to communicate is through the written word: writing each other love letters. If you wrote to each other frequently while you were dating and courting, you may have forgotten the power of the written word.

When was the last time you wrote something to each other besides a grocery list or a reminder to put the casserole in the oven? Try writing love letters or love notes. Put them on the pillow, perhaps with a rose, or in a lunchbox or briefcase. Don't put qualifications on your love notes, however. Give your expressions to each other free of expectations. Naturally, you would like to expect exciting results, but remain open. You give your love and your expressions of love freely and without strings attached: that is love.

Talk to each other about expanding your communication patterns, spicing them up with new styles. You should notice a decidedly positive effect on your marriage relationship. Enjoy it.

Make your communication a two-way street. Remember, you both have a right and a need to communicate. In many marriages, one spouse is more skilled as a communicator than the other spouse and may actually take over the communication process. Unfortunately, this can put an end to communication altogether because the less-skilled communicator starts to feel he or she doesn't stand a chance. The why-bother-to-try syndrome sets in. The result is likely to be anger, alienation, and distancing.

Give each other all the time and space necessary to communicate feelings, thoughts, and attitudes. When it comes to communication, don't hurry; communication is far too important a process to rush.

Don't assume: commune. If you've been married for many years, you may be inclined to believe that you know everything there is to know about each other. You may believe that you know what each other is thinking and may even make certain assumptions or decisions based on reading each other's mind.

This is really noncommunication and can be extremely damaging to your relationship.

No matter how well you know each other, no matter how long you've been together, you never really know what each other is thinking. Genuine communication demands true interaction between the two of you, not just making assumptions. God is the only one who reads the mind and heart, and that is the way it should be.

Change, adapt, and restructure communication patterns as the need arises. Perhaps what worked well for you five or ten years ago in terms of communication techniques is now threadbare; you find yourself frustrated or bored.

Give your communication machinery a tune-up. Change your style of relating to better meet your needs today; you will likely find your marriage significantly enriched.

If you take the time to learn how to communicate well, if you work at it during all the various moods and phases of your marriage, you will find yourselves in a strong and healthy marriage. You will withstand the storms of married life — all the while learning to better appreciate the special joys unique to your sacrament of marriage.

Do you not know that a little yeast leavens all the dough? Clear out the old yeast, so that you may become a fresh batch of dough....

1 Corinthians 5:6-7

⊙⊙ LACK OF QUALITY TIME TOGETHER

In the course of counseling couples, I notice that lack of quality time together frequently surfaces as a major relationship issue. Because it is mentioned so often, it merits our attention here.

Lack of quality time certainly deserves the label of marriage breaker: it creates a sense of distance and painful loneliness in the marriage. The unspoken message conveyed when the two of you fail to spend quality time together is "We're too busy to spend time with each other. We have more important things to do."

When this mentality creeps into your marriage, you can count on eventual estrangement. When the two of you fail to spend quality time together, your communication and intimacy deteriorate, your anger levels increase, and you'll find yourselves thinking, "We don't really know each other any-more."

This is what happened to Alex and Christine.

"When we were first married," Alex admits, "I loved spending time with Christine; the more the better. We had both quantity and quality time together, and our marriage flourished because of it.

"But after several years, I started to feel restless and bored and started neglecting the marriage. I began pulling away from Chris without realizing what was happening. Other women began to look better to me than Chris, and though I never so much as touched one of them, I committed emotional adultery in my mind again and again.

"I started spending less and less time at home and plunged into an endless round of activities. I joined a bowling team and a poker club, and I went fishing and golfing as often as I could.

"When Chris began to complain, I would point out to her that I was just relaxing with the boys and wasn't running around with any women, so how could she possibly be upset?

"Chris knew that I was running away from her, and she tried to get me to slow down and face things, but I ignored her. I ran as hard and as fast as I could, until one day she informed me that she had filed for divorce. That stopped me cold."

Alex pauses and grins. "When your wife tells you she's getting a divorce, it feels like someone has hit you over the head with a sledgehammer. Needless to say, she got my attention fast.

"I asked her for just one more chance — and with a lot of reservations, she finally agreed. We got counseling right away, and I really think it's helping.

"There are still times when I want to run from her and do

my own thing, but now I know how hard that is on our relationship. Now I stop and take time for her and us, and slowly, things are improving. I think we're going to save this marriage, thank God."

A Hollow Shell or a Precious Bond

A couple often takes far better care of their automobiles, their house, and their pet than they do their marriage. Does that sound like your relationship? A lack of quality time in your marriage is a clear sign that basic "marital maintenance" is being neglected — and the signs and consequences of that neglect will soon become evident.

Periodically, the two of you — together — need to stop and take a good look at the health of your marriage. This isn't something one of you does alone and then presents it to the other. This is a mutual exercise, a marital checkup that can help you detect problem areas — such as lack of quality time — before they seriously impair the well-being of your marriage. Children, jobs and careers, church involvements, community activities, hobbies and sports, family-of-origin concerns, pursuits of higher education, and friends are but a few of the common areas that begin to get your quality time. Anything left over from these investments is then brought to your marriage — which usually amounts to little more than crumbs of time. When the children are gone, work and careers are exhausted, church and community activities lose their meaning, hobbies and sports lose their appeal, family-of-origin concerns are resolved, educations are completed, and friends move on, there is nothing left but a hollow shell of something that was vibrant with mutual interests and good times together.

Irene agrees.

"I loved Jack a lot, but while we were married I loved the children more. I gave them everything: my time, my affection, my care, my love — you name it. The children turned out beautifully, but our marriage fell apart."

Why so?

"I really thought that the children made the marriage work. Now I know that a husband and wife make a marriage work. I gave Jack as much as I could, but it was like giving a person dying of thirst a few drops of water. The kids got all of me; Jack got a little of me, and it wasn't enough. He finally left.

"I guess marriage is a lot like a flower garden. If you don't give it the time and attention it needs, you'll lose it to the weeds, the bugs, the drought, or something. You've got to work on it and at it regularly or someday you'll find you don't have it anymore."

Lack of quality time may also be a form of avoidance behavior. One or both of you may attempt to dodge certain issues in your relationship by simply staying away or not getting too close to each other. The result, of course, is that certain issues simply never get resolved, and your relationship begins to lose life.

Do the two of you spend sufficient quality time together? If not, what are the marital issues you may be reluctant to face? The old saying goes, "You can run, but you can't hide." The very issues you are fleeing are likely to dog the heels of your marriage until they grow powerful enough to take a huge bite out of it. If you feel you want to face the issues and try for resolution but don't know where to begin, consider getting help in the form of professional counseling.

Most dramatically, lack of quality time takes its toll on your intimacy. Not just your sexual intimacy — although the result is likely to be that the two of you gradually become total strangers side by side in bed each night — but intimacy in the broad sense of being close.

When you cease to spend sufficient quality time together, you loose your sense of unity: you fail to remain close to each other. It's that simple — and that certain. Quality time allows for the development and deepening of intimacy. It allows your relationship to become solid and durable. The investment of quality time in your marriage is an investment that will last a lifetime. Remove it, and your precious bond will begin to crumble; irreversible damage is inevitable.

⊘ WORKING TOGETHER

Most of the following suggestions for increasing the quality time you spend together come directly from couples I've worked with. These suggestions have been field-tested and have been found to be effective. If you implement even one of them, quality time in your marriage relationship should improve.

Prioritize time together. Quality time can happen spontaneously, but there is nothing wrong in planning it as well. Take and make time for each other as often as you possibly can.

For example, can the two of you (and only the two of you) take a vacation together? If not a full vacation, how about a weekend alone together? If not a weekend, what about a night away together? You can't afford it? Okay, how about a day spent together somewhere? If a full day is not workable, at least a few hours: walk, talk, be with each other. If you absolutely cannot get away from the house, agree to a block of time that is strictly yours: retreat to your bedroom and allow no phone calls or interruptions from the kids.

This may sound like you're being selfish or irresponsible parents — but you're not. You're being sane. The children are not going to become juvenile delinquents or suffer from permanent fear of abandonment just because the two of you arrange time together without them. These kinds of concerns often come from an overidentification with the kids on the part of the parent rather than a genuine concern for the good of the children.

If you're not willing to make time together a priority, or if you spout an endless list of reasons the two of you can't find time alone together, you're undoubtedly running away from closeness in your marriage. Before your relationship suffers irreversible damage, find out what you're running from and why.

Be creative. There are no patterns or master plans for the two of you to follow. You are the only ones who can determine what quality time is for your marriage. Your quality time is not going to look like the quality time another couple might prefer or need.

For example, some couples resume dating each other. They may enjoy a movie together, dinner and dancing, a Saturday evening picnic, a drive in the country. They make these arrangements ahead of time and enjoy the excitement of anticipation.

For other couples, quality time means everything from a camping trip together to holding hands while riding in the car to watching the sun set to pausing to say a prayer before leaving for work.

Quality time is anything and everything you choose to make it. There is no one best model that is appropriate for every married couple. Once you determine what works for you, avail yourselves of it as often as you can and watch your sense of closeness grow.

Celebrate your anniversaries. An anniversary provides a ready-made opportunity for quality time together. You don't have to spend a lot of money, just celebrate it a special way.

Renew your marriage vows on your wedding anniversary. Join hands and, once again, pledge your love, trust, and fidelity to each other. You don't need a priest or minister to witness this sacred moment; bless each other, bless your rings, and bless the life you share. Spend quiet time together reflecting on the years behind you — and ahead of you. Share your disappointments, your joys, your dreams.

Celebrate your wedding anniversary every month. If you were married on the twenty-first of the month, make the twenty-first of every month special in some small way, even if it's just a simple lunch at a local fast-food restaurant or an intimate cup of mocha late in the evening.

Plan a care day each week. Select one day each week to be your care day. On this day, you both have the right to ask each other for one reasonable favor that includes time alone. You may want to ask for a back rub right before bed, a little extra time in the morning before the kids get up, or a late night walk around the block.

Care days provide wonderful opportunities for quality time because they help you identify and respond to each other's needs. Try the care-day technique for one month; see how it impacts your relationship. If you like the results, keep it up...hopefully forever.

Be open to new experiences. Remain flexible and maintain a sense of adventure. Your husband wants to try a weekend of backpacking in the mountains, but you're terrified of snakes. Well, snakes are terrified of you. Give it a try. You may have a terrific time.

Your wife wants to browse the craft display, but you think it's all just a bunch of junk and clutter. Go with her; let her show you the fine handiwork in the items, the art involved in creating patterns and working with natural resources. It could be more exciting than you ever thought possible — and think of how you will be pleasing her. Quality time can generate memories that last a lifetime.

You can also learn a great deal about quality time from other married couples. Ask your married friends what works for them. Couples who are happily married didn't get that way by accident; they built a happy marriage, together, with the mortar of quality time. Try to find out exactly what they did. Perhaps their secrets of success will work for you as well.

Don't allow the lack of quality time to become a marriage breaker in your relationship. You can neglect each other and your relationship — and pay the consequences for that neglect. Or you can use the time you spend together to enrich and enhance your marital relationship and transform it into something fulfilling, blessed, and long-lasting.

"O my dove in the clefts of the rock, / in the secret recesses of the cliff, / Let me see you, / let me hear your voice, / For your voice is sweet, / and you are lovely."

Song of Songs 2:14

⃝⃝ STINKIN' THINKIN'

It's not the situation that matters — or so say the ancient Greek philosophers. It's what we *think* about it that makes all the difference. While I do not espouse this axiom completely, those ancients must have moonlighted as marriage counselors when they weren't explaining the mysteries of the universe.

The way you think vastly affects your marital relationship. This chapter consists of common complaints couples bring to their counseling sessions — complaints I refer to as "stinkin' thinkin'."

Thoughts, behaviors, and feelings impact one another like the bumper-car ride at an amusement park; the turning, stopping, and jerking of one car can affect all the others. Likewise, a change in any one thought, behavior, or feeling can cause a ripple effect throughout the whole marital system. For example, lies, half-truths, exaggerations, and perpetual pessimism can produce a host of uncomfortable feelings, such as anxiety, depression, panic, anger, paranoia, and self-pity. Thoughts not grounded in reality make individuals and couples act a little crazy: pouting, throwing things, running away from home, binging to compensate, using sex as a weapon, and many other behaviors.

Patterns of Stinkin' Thinkin'

Thoughts are automatic, habitual, and preconscious — but they need not wield destructive power in your relationship. The following kinds of thinking are marriage breakers in any marital relationship. Read each section carefully and ask yourselves if anything sounds familiar. Undoubtedly, you can add more to this list, but these give you the general nature of what stinkin' thinkin' is and the havoc it can wreak. When you wrest these thought patterns from your relating, relief is — literally — a thought away.

All-or-nothing thinking: Pamela has a deep conversion experience. She is "born again," "saved," and almost "raptured" at a Catholic revival service. She becomes so passionate about spreading the Faith that her neighbors recommend she take aspirin and get plenty of bed rest.

Prior to her conversion experience, Pamela had been a fairly "regular" Catholic. She and her husband, Mike, attended Mass together every week and on holy days. Pamela wasn't indifferent to her Catholic faith, but she didn't run around proclaiming "Jesus is Lord." Mike was quiet about his faith, uncomfortable with any exuberant displays of religious passion. But after Pamela's conversion experience, Mike was in for quite a bit of religious passion.

Pamela coaches Mike to pray in tongues; she lays hands on him for inner healing; she shouts at him in an attempt to drive the evil forces from his soul. But Mike remains just an ordinary Catholic: no speaking in tongues, no instant healings, no profound experiences of a redeeming nature. Mike remains his quiet, prayerful, and sincere self.

Meanwhile, Pamela continues to act like she needs yet another conversion. She makes herself miserable because Mike doesn't share her spiritual zeal. She stops going to Mass with him so she can join a more Spirit-filled worship service in another parish, and she is gone several nights each week to attend prayer groups and Bible-study sessions. She desperately wants Mike to share in her ardor, but he is uncomfortable with her exuberance.

Pamela's outlook is an example of all-or-nothing thinking. She wants her husband to experience his faith the way she experiences her faith. She will settle for nothing short of the sparkly vitality she knows to be the fire of the Spirit in her own soul. If Mike can't display that, then he obviously is not devout in his faith.

Pamela's bullying, impatience, and arrogance rest on that pattern of stinkin' thinkin' called all-or-nothing. Eventually, Pamela seeks help when her prayers for Mike to "catch up" to her are not answered.

With pad and pencil in hand, Pamela begins to list the dutiful, thoughtful, and faithful practices of her husband's faith. In counseling, it is pointed out to her that many married Catholic women lead a lonely spiritual life because their husbands experience their faith in less dramatic ways. Many would give anything to share a prayer, a liturgy, or a conversation about God with their spouse.

Pamela begins to calm herself with more balanced thoughts: "Mike is a good man. The Lord does matter to him." She focuses on his gentleness and realizes that her forceful efforts have not been supportive of the unique way he lives his faith — a way that is "right" for him.

Pamela and Mike's marriage eventually returns to normal, and normal is really pretty good.

Mind reading: "I can read him like a book." "If she loves me, she knows I don't like that!" "I know what he's thinking, and as usual, he's wrong!"

Have you thought these thoughts? The fact is, most of us are not mind readers. Yes, many of us can recognize nonverbal cues with a fair amount of accuracy after years of intimate sharing. We might even have great skill in detective work, like Angela Lansbury in *Murder She Wrote.* But as a rule, we do not have psychic powers. We cannot read the thoughts of another; we cannot assume what the other is feeling.

In my work with couples, I insist that a spouse ask, "What did you mean by that?" — especially when the initial interpretation is a negative one.

Was it a bad day at the office? Did the baby spit up on the neighbor's new carpet? Are the credit cards causing panic? Is one of you uptight about weight gain, creeping baldness, or advancing age? These things float around in the back of your minds and are part of the baggage you bring to every exchange. They may have nothing to do with the issue at hand, yet they "color" responses, causing one or both of you to be cross, impatient, or defensive. Aloofness or absent-mindedness may be strongly irritating behaviors, but they hardly constitute grounds for concluding that an affair is going on right under your nose. Your marriage will gradually be eroded with this kind of stinkin' thinkin'.

Begin today to release your marriage from the stranglehold of mind reading. You are each changing every minute of your lives. Experience and time cause you to shift preferences, opinions, and even patterns of behavior. Love each other enough to allow those shifts to develop naturally. Do not build a box around each other's personhood by assuming you know what he or she is thinking, feeling, needing, doing. Ask questions: "May I ask what you're thinking?" "Is there anything you'd like to talk about?"

Don't wait until the kids are grown and gone (and are beginning to return to drop off their own kids) to inventory your mind-reading patterns. What are things you automatically assume about each other? Become aware of these particular assumptions and consciously dismiss them when they begin to influence your own thinking.

Labeling: She stormed into the office with fire in her eyes, threw herself in a chair, and pointed at the young man sheepishly entering the room behind her.

"He's immature!"

He shamefacedly proceeded to slink into the chair farthest away from her, then murmured, "Yup, she's right. I'm immature."

When this couple entered counseling, their primary task was to learn a new language. Certainly, the young man had to grow up; don't we all. But calling him "immature" defined him, and his acceptance of that title imprisoned him.

Ten times during that first conversation in my office, the man's wife used the word *immature,* and each time the beaten man in the chair slumped deeper. His wife saw no hope for the marriage since the stress was unbearable. He didn't help with their two young children; he didn't help with household chores; he didn't help with the tedious responsibility of managing the household budget; he didn't take seriously his efforts to find a job.

A new pair of glasses had to be issued to this young couple. The wife needed to see her husband in a different light, to turn loose of the crushing label "immature." The husband, in turn, needed to see himself with his own eyes instead of allowing his wife to give him a definition.

One of the first things the husband had to do was find a good teacher, someone who could teach him some basics about homeowning. He connected with a mentor, an old uncle, who taught him simple mechanical know-how. The wife softened as she took notice of her husband's efforts to learn. She even discovered her own patience to explain routine childcare measures and budgeting tactics. Her self-applied label of "nag" quickly faded.

Each week, this couple reported some kind of progress. During our sessions together, the husband sat up straighter as he listed the small chores he was beginning to master around the house. The wife glanced at her husband with a soft, affectionate smile instead of a scowl. During the final session, she sat close to him, holding his hand.

What power in a label!

Do you limit each other with nicknames or terms that crush the spirit? The God of Scripture distinguishes between the doer and the deed. Some of me is not all of me. None of us is finished yet.

As I officiate at weddings, I often wonder about the decorations on the wedding car: old shoes, beer cans, and toilet paper. I read the taunts: "Bite the dust," "Tie the knot," "Hitched." All of these symbols and labels paint a poor picture of marriage right from the start.

In one of the Scripture readings for a wedding Mass, Jesus gives his disciples two labels: "salt of the earth" and "light of the world." More than anyone, he knew the power of labels that build, create, affirm, and nurture the good in others. You long remember what you hear each other say. What, indeed, are you saying? How are you saying it? How does your labeling of each other affect your marriage?

Should've-would've-could've thinking: We learn a lot by looking back over our shoulder at what's behind us. Regrets have an especially strong impact on us. When we realize that an opportunity has been lost, we fall into the "should've-would've-could've" pattern of stinkin' thinkin'.

How often I've heard these comments from widows or widowers: "I should've said 'I love you!'" "We should've gone on that trip instead of waiting for retirement." "If only I could've had a second chance!" "I would've proven to you that we could do it, if we'd just had more time." "I could've been a better spouse if I had tried harder!"

There's wisdom in these words borne of pain and loss. As long as people still breathe, there is hope! The married living waste too much time and energy bemoaning the mistakes and sins of their past. The regrets are gifts if they're viewed as moments of life instead of moments of loss. The Christian response to sin is repentance and a firm purpose of amendment. A little guilt for the right reasons can facilitate change. On the other hand, too much guilt over too little too late will paralyze.

Nancy and Bob salt their wounds regularly with this unholy tirade. "I should've known better than to invest so much of our savings in that now-defunct business." Bob kicks himself and then begs Nancy to kick him as well.

Nancy, on the other hand, had wanted to argue against the risk; at the time, she didn't think it was a wise and safe investment. But she had kept quiet — and now she tortures herself for her timidity. "I could've been more assertive. I should've insisted he not invest so much when the risks were so high."

"What would've happened if we'd hung on to our nest egg?" they moan. "Maybe we'd quit arguing. Maybe our financial worries would lighten. If only...if only...if only...."

In counseling, Nancy and Bob are learning to analyze their mistakes so as to avoid similar pitfalls in the future. They are coached in problem-solving: the art of generating solutions and periodically reevaluating them. They're learning the "win-win" stance of conflict resolution.

They're learning quickly — and as they learn, their anger is beginning to subside. Their marriage is healing.

It is refreshing to watch a married couple free themselves from the mire of self-pity. It is also a grace-filled event to see a couple like Nancy and Bob liberate themselves as they forgive each other and themselves and move together into a future filled with new energy and hope.

Love mania: Songs claim we can't live without it, and movies keep us titillated by the "fatal attraction" of it.

The Bible, too, is replete with references to love. As gospel people, we believe that God is Love — that Love became flesh in Jesus Christ. We're even treated to the sweet surprise of romantic and erotic images of love sprinkled throughout the Scriptures.

Yet, there is a difference between the love talk of God's Word and the smothering soap-operish version that many couples believe they must maintain to remain happy. Love mania is seeking after and insisting on the smothering, passion-ridden, and never-ending excitement of love — and that kind of "love" is destructive and dangerous.

So often we witness couples promising to love each other through the years: when wrinkles set in, when pennies are pinched, when bodies grow frail, and when major setbacks make life especially difficult. But how many couples, do you suppose, keep their fingers crossed when they declare these vows? How many couples think ahead to the realities of ten, thirty, and fifty years from their wedding day?

Bill had a belly on him, and Rose was thirty pounds overweight. Bill was hard-of-hearing, and Rose snored. Sex was no longer dynamic; no bells or fireworks anymore. It was just simple, gentle, comfortable — and satisfying.

Bill and Rose began reading the pop-love books and magazines and taking literally all the sensuous promises suggested by commercials for certain coffees, deodorants, cereals, and toothpastes. They were satisfied and content, but they let popular thinking convince them there should be more "magic" in their relationship. They were looking for ways to put heat back into their relationship.

Their complaint was common.

During counseling, Bill and Rose were reminded of the all-important question Tevye asks his wife, Golde, in that beautiful play, *Fiddler on the Roof.* Tevye asks Golde if she loves him. Her reply is that for twenty-five years she has lived with him, fought with him, starved with him, shared his bed, taken care of him, the house, the kids, and has milked the cow...and if that's not love, what is?

The ordinary moments of married life have their own magic: a good-morning kiss, a lingering cup of coffee together, help with the dishes, waiting together in the doctor's office, a surprise card, that special dessert, a casual but sincere compliment. Every bit of this is love.

The notion of love mania, although promulgate in our culture, is a myth. As your marriage matures, you will grow to appreciate dull and routine as indeed beautiful, and uneventful as extraordinary. The cross is the prerequisite for resurrection even — no, *especially* — in a Christian marriage.

⊘ WORKING TOGETHER

There are three simple guidelines to follow in canceling stinkin' thinkin' from your thought patterns. Make these a habit of your conscious thinking and give your relationship a coat of armor against the ravages of negative thinking that can erode your marriage.

Avoid making assumptions. Your marriage is not only based on love for each other but it is also rooted in the grace of a sacrament. Do not abuse your relationship by assuming anything. Recall that this is one of the communication skills mentioned in a previous chapter. Give each other a chance to explain circumstances, share feelings, and explain behavior. What you don't know will hurt you — so ask questions! If you do assume, assume the best! Give each other the benefit of the doubt in every situation.

Attempt to be objective. Insufficient objectivity in an intimate relationship leads to myopic vision and closed minds. To every set of circumstances, there are many valid perspectives, perspectives that are fashioned by moods, histories, and personal values. Don't shut out each other by clinging to your own subjective point of view. Give your spouse and yourself a special opportunity to stretch and grow by ripping off the blinders of subjective thinking and embracing objectivity.

Bless every moment. Any given moment of your life together is part of the mortar that holds your marriage together. Because you want only the strongest ingredients in that mortar, careful attention must be given to every minute. To wish the moment would pass, to wish an incident hadn't happened, to long for some other set of circumstances, is to neglect the gift of potential life in the immediate moment. Frustration sets in and stinkin' thinkin' is given a strong foothold. Don't let that happen. This moment is a crucial link to the rest of your life; give it your undivided attention.

"...your kingdom come. / Give us each day our daily bread / and forgive us our sins / for we ourselves forgive everyone in debt to us, / and do not subject us to the final test. "

Luke 11:2-4

∞ LACK OF SHARED SPIRITUAL VALUES

Many couples ignore or neglect the spiritual dimension of their relationship — to the detriment of their marriage.

A lack of common spiritual values is a severe marriage breaker. It robs your marriage of perhaps the most valuable tool there is for cementing a lasting relationship, a tool that provides you with the inner resources for coping with crises while enabling you to build genuine intimacy.

Simply put, the tool is *a relationship with God* — along with the development of a sound spirituality of marriage. Although it sounds like a cliché, a relationship with God and developing a sound spirituality of marriage means letting God truly be the third Partner in your marriage.

Keeping God out of your marriage will prevent you from fully realizing the powerful potential of love and grace in your relationship. Without God as your third Partner, you will eventually begin to know a nagging, empty, impoverished vacuum within. Growth and life will not happen; love will not flourish. A marriage without God is a needy marriage, indeed.

Gary agrees.

"I was a cradle Catholic, but I never took my faith seriously. My parents saw to it that I made my first Communion and was confirmed, and of course, my marriage to Therese took place in the Church. But for a good part of my life, the practice of religion was a way of pleasing others, like my mom and dad. I might as well have been a Druid, worshiping oak trees and the stars, for all the good it did me. I never really put my heart into it.

"I didn't have a personal relationship with God at all. I saw God as some kind of Santa Claus in the sky, someone I could go to when I wanted something. So when the first major crisis of our marriage hit, I was unprepared to handle it. I literally fell apart."

What was the crisis?

"Therese and I had both looked forward to having a baby. We knew we would be good parents. In the second year of our marriage, our first child was born — a gorgeous little girl. A week after we brought her home, she died of sudden infant death syndrome. I'm the one who found her.

"Therese and I were both plunged into the kind of grieving we had heard about but never thought possible. The difference between us, though, is that she started to work through her grief right away. She joined a bereavement group at church and started to see a counselor. She began to heal, but I didn't."

What happened?

"I stuffed my grief way down inside of me. Therese tried her best to help me; she tried to get me to talk about it and invited me to pray with her. But I just couldn't do that; God was a total stranger to me. So I ignored her — and I ignored God. I finally started to find some solace, though…in a bottle."

Gary shakes his head in amazement. "I'm really surprised that I'm still here. I became so self-destructive with my drinking that I must have wanted to die more than I realized at the time. Nothing and no one mattered. I just wanted the pain inside to stop.

"Therese begged me over and over again to get help, but I denied there was a problem. Finally, she moved back home with her parents. Then I was really alone, and it wasn't long before I was close to going over the edge once and for all."

What turned things around?

Gary smiles. "It was the grace of God! God literally gave me a second chance. I was coming home from a bar one evening, smashed out of my mind as usual, but driving my car anyway, drunken idiot that I was. A little girl ran out into the street, chasing a ball, and I hit her.

"Thank God, I didn't kill her. I ended up in jail for drunk driving, though, and when I got out, I went straight into inpatient treatment for alcoholism. The thought of a little girl dead because of me scared me sober, but I still needed professional help. And in the recovery program, I met God for the first time.

"God really does work in mysterious ways. Alcoholics Anonymous calls God a Higher Power and Higher Friend — and I've found both titles to be true. God saved my life and my marriage. Once Therese saw how hard I was trying, she came back, and the two of us invited God into our marriage to stay."

Gary laughs. "That was fifteen years ago. We have three

children now, and it's been a good and happy marriage. But I believe with all my heart and soul that neither I nor the marriage would be here today without God's help. And Therese and I are grateful for that gift every single day."

The Ties That Bind

Spiritual values are literally the ties that bind a married couple to each other. When everything else seems to be collapsing, the spiritual life of a marriage is the foundation that holds everything together — including the relationship. Without shared spiritual values, spouses are likely to discover that their marriage is built on sand and not on rock, especially when the going gets rough. Because our culture emphasizes exciting romance over spiritual growth and strength, married couples often fail to realize and recognize that the lack of a marital spirituality is directly linked to intimacy deprivation.

Intimacy can be broadly defined as the "state of being close." In the Catholic view of marriage, intimacy is considered to be so important that the Second Vatican Council actually described marriage as an "intimate partnership" (*Pastoral Constitution on the Church in the Modern World*, #49). Undergirded by love, trust, and fidelity, this is the essence of the married covenant.

Our society would have us believe that intimacy is achieved primarily — perhaps even exclusively — through the sexual expression that takes place between the spouses. In reality, intimacy has strong psychological, emotional, and spiritual components as well as the physical. Remove any one of these, and marital intimacy suffers. Again and again, I have observed that those couples who actively and deliberately cultivate and nurture a strong spiritual life achieve a level of intimacy denied couples who place no importance in a spirituality of marriage.

Soul-mate Intimacy

You will not know yourselves as soul mates unless together you nurture and nourish the life of each other's soul, which is primarily a spiritual entity. That means sustaining and maintaining a relationship with the living God who has breathed life into your souls and bodies and who brought the two of you together in wisdom and providence.

If you really want to be close, if you want the deepest possible intimacy, the two of you need to walk with God as well as each other, sharing your faith life and faith experiences with each other. Keeping your spiritual life private and personal, never letting your spouse get a glimpse of it, will cause you to miss the richest, most sacred purpose of marriage. Marriage is designed by God to help the two of you grow and mature spiritually — together. Only as soul mates can you fully embrace the depths and mysteries of your covenant. You are both deprived when you neglect the spiritual reality of what your relationship is all about — and your marriage remains at risk.

God's grace is given as a gift to help sanctify the two of you. Thus, in your shared life, Christ the Lord is more visible. If you hoard your faith and withhold your spiritual experiences from each other, how is this to happen? Shared faith leads to greater intimacy than you can believe possible. Recall the walk to Emmaus following the crucifixion of Jesus. In sharing their faith along the journey, the two companions were able to welcome Christ into their very midst — and, indeed, recognize him. (See Luke 24:13-35.) You discover this great truth only by living it.

Elaine and Harold have been married sixty years. They are a lovely and loving couple. Their faith lies at the center of their long marriage, and they make that clear without being ostentatious about it.

"My goodness, yes!" exclaims Elaine, her eyes twinkling. "On our wedding day, we committed our married life to God, and every single day we make that commitment all over again. In the morning, we start off with a prayer together, placing the day in God's hands. Then, just before bedtime, we pray together, thanking God for all our blessings — the ones we know about and the ones we won't know about until we see God face to face."

Harold nods his head in agreement. "Being believers in God and being husband and wife are one and the same to us. We couldn't imagine being married without sharing our faith with each other — and really with everyone we come in touch with. That's what faith is meant for — to be given away, starting with the persons closest to you, the ones right in your own home."

If the two of you deepen your walk with the Lord, the intimacy you share will deepen, your friendship and love for each other and others will grow, you will become the soul mates you were meant to be, and your marriage will be richer and more fulfilling than you ever thought possible.

WORKING TOGETHER

The following methods for enriching and deepening your spiritual life have proven helpful for other couples. Some of them will work for you.

Pray together and stay together. I often ask couples — those engaged to be married and those who have come to me for marriage counseling — if they ever pray together. The couples either look at me as though I've just arrived from another planet, or they start stammering about having to leave because of another urgent commitment.

When it comes to prayer, couples get nervous or embarrassed — or both. Spiritual intimacy is likely to make them far more uncomfortable than physical intimacy. Baring your body is easy compared to baring your soul.

The fact is that intimacy is a by-product of shared prayer. Traditional prayers are valuable, but they don't have the bonding power that spontaneous, heartfelt, tear-filled, laughter-filled, and soul-filled praying has.

Try this form of prayer. Take each other's hand, become aware of God's presence, and simply talk to God in your own words — together. Make your prayer one of deep thanksgiving and praise for God's many blessings to the two of you and your family. Make it a prayer of petition for your marriage, for the marriage of others, and for those you know who are in need of the spiritual energy your love generates.

You may need to use your prayer time to pray for reconciliation. Couples frequently hurt and wound each other. By praying for and extending forgiveness with a kiss or a hug, you can rapidly resolve a great deal of anger and bring much healing to your relationship — before the hurt begins to fester.

Marge laughs. "Steve and I have been married forty-five years. There were some days when we battled like crazy, and during those times, I dearly wanted to hold a grudge and get a chance to enjoy my anger at him. But just before going to bed, we've always prayed together."

"Yes," Steve chimes in with a chuckle, "and I remind her that the Lord says we have to forgive seventy-seven times. So we always kiss and make up."

Marge throws up her hands. "What chance do I have against

him and the Lord?" She reaches over and squeezes Steve's hand. "Especially when they're right!"

Worship together. It isn't unusual for me to witness the marriage of a couple and then not see them in church again until Christmas, Easter, or perhaps someone else's wedding.

Worshiping together with a believing faith community is a powerful means for not only strengthening marital bonds but also for unifying the entire family.

Fundamentally, Christianity is a social religion. We cannot live our faith in isolation from others. As we join with other Christians in worship of God, we find both spiritual support and social support from the community of believers who recognize and affirm the importance of marriage and family.

If you are not a member of your local parish church, consider registering and regularly worshiping there. The parish has been called the "neighborhood Christ." The Lord awaits you there with special graces that flow through sacramental life as it is experienced *in community.*

Draw upon other spiritual resources. In most communities, there are a variety of spiritual resources that the two of you can rely on to enrich and invigorate your marriage.

Check your local parish for details, dates, and places for Marriage Encounter weekends. Make a retreat together. Your parish can help you locate retreats that are being offered. Even if you have to travel some distance, go. This kind of experience must be prioritized for the strength of your marriage.

Join a prayer group or a Bible-study group. If your parish offers days or evenings of recollection and reflection for married couples, take advantage of these opportunities to nurture your common faith journey.

Celebrate Mass together on a weekday morning and afterward go for breakfast. When the two of you cultivate a deeper relationship with God and share the fruits which flow from that relationship, your marriage is blessed, healed, enriched, renewed, and enlivened. Intimacy is deepened as a direct result of your efforts to be open to God's grace.

Be open to new ways of experiencing your spirituality. Some couples begin and end the day with some small ritual, something as simple as tenderly blessing each other with the Sign of the Cross on the forehead to bring them into a conscious awareness of God as their third Partner. Other couples establish a regular prayer time together; they pray a psalm each day, alternating the verses. Since there are one hundred and fifty psalms, that's about five months of prayer material!

Some couples discuss the Sunday homily, a Scripture passage, or something they've read that pertains to faith. Be creative: the realm of the Spirit is rich and varied. Greater spiritual creativity, variety, and experimentation will enrich your walk with the Lord in surprising ways — if you'll simply trust yourselves to God's grace.

The lack of common spiritual values and a shared spirituality in marriage is an inevitable marriage breaker. It deprives a marriage of all the invaluable resources that not only enrich the marital relationship but also help protect it against the stresses and strains that sooner or later beset every marriage.

A relationship with God and a marital spirituality are not achieved overnight. Both need to be consciously and deliberately constructed by the investment of time and spiritual energy.

Once the two of you have achieved a shared spiritual life with God's help, remember the need for maintenance. That means using the many spiritual resources and tools available to you for that purpose.

As you grow spiritually, you will grow in other ways as well. Your marriage will be bountifully blessed and become something beautiful not only for yourselves but also for the God who has brought you together and bonded you together as friends, partners, and lifelong gifts to each other.

"Were not our hearts burning [within us] while he spoke to us on the way and opened the scriptures to us?"

Luke 24:32

PART II

∞

MARRIAGE
MAKERS

⃝⃝ INTRODUCTION

The central idea evident in Part I is that a crack in the marital foundation, although cause for grave concern, *can* be patched before a major collapse occurs. Anger, poor communication skills, lack of quality time together, stinkin' thinkin', and lack of shared spiritual values are, indeed, threats to the bond you share. Working together, the two of you can help each other minimize these threats.

In my contribution to Part I — the chapter on stinkin' thinkin' — I pointed out faulty thinking and suggested a more realistic and compassionate way to view each other. In Part II, I go a step further, a step higher; I suggest practical, workable approaches that will enhance the *making* of a good marriage.

If you experiment with any of these strategies, you will see positive results. A change in thought, emotion, or behavior in small, positive directions has far-reaching repercussions. Little successes add up.

Living marriage as a sacrament, the two of you have access to tremendous spiritual resources that will support you in enriching and renewing your relationship. The Lord has a vested interest in your union, you know. God covenanted with you on your wedding day, even if you were too nervous or too preoccupied to appreciate it.

Although I pen the content of the following chapters, in all honesty it is not my material. It is the wisdom of married couples like you, couples who are willing to invest a lifetime in making their relationship sacramentally healthy and satisfying, thus reflecting the life of Christ in our midst. I am indebted to the married couples who have helped me appreciate the vocation of my own sacramental call; I hope the following material reflects my awe at theirs.

Jack Leipert

∞ EXCEPTIONS AND MIRACLES

Sometimes solutions are right under our noses. One does not have to unearth the hidden, unconscious meaning of family histories and behaviors to save a marriage. Blowing the dust off a few good memories will often do the trick.

Couples who come for counseling are frequently jolted into hope by an opening question such as "Since you called for an appointment, what's gone right in your relationship that you want to keep happening?"

So preoccupied with what is wrong, so determined to blame and complain, the couple cannot perceive that some healthy change has probably already happened. With a little prodding, however, the couple usually starts to perk up as they recall even a modicum of improvement: "Well, she's less tense since we took the first step in asking for help." "He's now talking to me in complete sentences. In fact, we didn't stop talking all the way over here."

I will then ask, "Do you like this change?"

"Yes!" invariably is the response.

"Think of what you have accomplished within a short time just by deciding to pick up the phone. You should congratulate yourselves. Remember what you did differently this time so that we can use this new behavior as a resource later."

The Exception Becomes the Norm

With a little close attention, the exception can become the norm, replacing the "woe-is-me" syndrome with an atmosphere of optimism. And you can do it without any professional coaching, once you know what to look for.

Sal and Sophie have been married forty-five years and have eight kids. They came for counseling, complaining of no "whoopee" in their sex life. They "did" sex once a month, religiously, but the flutter and thrill was gone from the experience.

"We've been reading that we shouldn't be too pooped to pucker, even at our age," Sophie explained. "Can you 'fix' us, especially since the doctor claims we're able? We're just not ready and willing anymore."

"Anymore" was the key. The word *anymore* implies there was a time the couple were, indeed, ready and willing, when puckering must have flourished. Sophie and Sal simply needed to remember the exception.

"Tell me, do the two of you remember a time when your sex life was passionate?"

Sophie blushed and nudged Sal. "Go ahead. Tell him."

Sal rolled back his eyes, put his fist to his chin, and took a quick trip down memory lane. Finally, he smiled and spoke.

"Sophie and I used to go joy ridin' in the country during those first years of marriage. I remember those back roads, the excitement, the fear of being caught. We dared them to catch us. After all, we were married. We even had the rings to prove it."

Sophie blushed some more, and Sal sighed at the thought of what had once been so much fun. The missing ingredient in their life of intimacy together was spontaneity and perhaps a bit of intrigue.

I gave the couple some homework; each night for a week, they were to find an old back road or lover's lane and let the sparks fly.

Sal and Sophie bounced into my office a week later, a giggling couple looking somewhat sheepish but much younger. It was soon clear that they had recaptured the magic — and perhaps even learned a few new tricks. They had remembered the exception and put it to work for them.

Bret and Brenda had no use for each other. Disgust was too mild a word to describe the pained look on their faces as they came to counseling for one last try to save their marriage. Both were zealous church workers who believed in involvement — except with each other.

"Do you remember a time recently when the two of you felt even a tinge of connection?"

"Maybe a month ago," replied Brenda, "when the painter we hired botched the job. We looked at each other, rolled up our sleeves, and got to work trying to fix the mess."

Bret nodded. "It took us awhile, but we got the job done. You know, we have plenty of money and help lots of people, and, individually, we take on the world. But it had been years since we'd tackled a project together. I guess those hours slaving over a common task felt good. We hadn't been that close in a long time — and we haven't been that close since."

Without realizing it, Bret and Brenda had surfaced the solution to their estrangement by remembering the exception. The next step was obvious; we lined up projects that required teamwork, whether at home or at church. The blues soon lifted as the couple actually began to experience happiness in working together.

In Part I, lack of quality time was highlighted as a major marriage breaker. The other side of that coin holds true as well; quality time together is an effective marriage maker. But only the two of you know what that quality time should look like, what works best for your relationship. Often you'll suffer from temporary amnesia about what makes you happy as a couple. Once that amnesia lifts, however, and you're willing to invest the creative energy into capturing the exception, the happiness can return.

A sixteen-year-old youngster and his parents hustled into the counseling office. The father was red with rage; the mother was frustrated. The child shuffled to the far corner of the office and dumped himself into a chair.

According to the couple, their son was ruining their marriage. They claimed to have tried everything. She had cried with hysteria; he had lectured with stern determination. Nothing seemed to work. How could the child not heed his mother's tears and his father's stern lectures? Where were they going wrong? It seemed to the parents that the situation was the opposite of child abuse; the couple felt they were being abused by the child.

The sixteen-year-old sat sullenly against the wall while his parents glared at each other with a "he's-your-kid" look. A former angelic altar boy had turned into a demon warrior from hell.

Remembering the exception was crucial to this family. We began walking down memory lane. "Can you recall a time when your son put down his dukes and, despite himself, listened to you?"

The father snarled, "That's a crazy question! He just needs to know who makes the rules. He'll never make it in the real world if he doesn't. You've got to have ambition and drive! This kid has about as much oomph as a wet noodle."

"Nevertheless," I pushed, "try to remember even one time, be it ever so brief, when the chemistry clicked for the two of you."

The father thought for a moment, glanced over at his son, and then spoke in a quiet tone. "About a year ago, we went on a biking trip. I was razzing him about keeping up with the old man, since he doesn't have much stomach for toughing things out. While chewing him out, I took my eye off the gravel road in front of me. Before I knew what happened, I flipped the bike, landed on the gravel, and ripped open my knee. I even cried. My boy there came to the rescue.

"At first, I resented his help. I don't like looking weak, especially in front of my family. But I was in pretty bad shape, and after a bit, the whole scene struck me as being kind of funny. I started laughing — and I laughed until I started crying again. Then he started laughing, and there we were, the two of us laughing our heads off."

I asked for more.

"Well, then we started talking. I mean we really talked — we really relaxed and enjoyed each other. For a few minutes we were equals. He even told me about some things that had been bugging him for a long time. There's been so much tension between us these past months that I'd nearly blocked that incident completely from my mind."

After peeling away the harsh talk, lo and behold, Dad was human. That remembering, that exception to the rule, contained the seeds of success for this family's healing. The boy could relate to a fallible father, not someone trying to be superdad.

After that revelation, we set up a few projects, projects familiar to the son but somewhat foreign to the father. The two were instructed to work on these projects together. In the weeks that followed, several successful interactions took place between father and child. The teenage son opened up, sought advice, and even taught his old man a few new skills. In turn, the father actually began to enjoy his son's company. Father and son began to respect each other's special gifts — and limitations.

The parent-child transformation helped the marriage as well. The man's wife saw a tender side of her husband that she had forgotten existed. It was a quality she had admired in the early years of their relationship. Remembering the exceptions triggered a chain reaction.

WORKING TOGETHER

You don't need a counselor to help you remember the moments in your relationship that were exciting and sweet. Those memories are part of the foundation on which your marriage rests today. Dig in there and celebrate the exceptions.

Remember the early — very early — stage of your relationship. Your early days, weeks, months, and years were special. You simply thought, felt, and acted differently. Recall those exceptional moments; they hold a treasure that can serve you now. Even a small piece of your happiest marital history can put you in touch with the embers within, embers that can warm you today and invite you into renewal.

Remember how you became engaged? Was it an impulse? How much romance was there? What made you blush or giggle in those first encounters? Recall the perfume or cologne that drove you wild. Is it still on the market?

What kind of music did the two of you like? Did you dance to a favorite song? Dig up that old recording and once more croon your special love song to each other.

Did you have a special place? a restaurant, drive-in, park, bar? Share what you remember about that place. What did it look like? What made it special? Is it possible to return there? If not, return there in your mind. See how the memories wait there to delight you and embrace you.

And can you ever forget those thrilling words, "We're going to have a baby"? What was that first pregnancy like for the two of you? Have you ever shared exactly how you felt during those long months of waiting? Were you excited? fearful? confident? confused? What did it feel like the first time you were able to say to yourself, "We are parents"? Remember the miracle of that child's birth. Was it a time of rejoicing or a time of grief? Were there complications? Have you ever shared deeply what that first birth meant to you? No doubt, you each experienced things differently.

Remember.

What were those early jobs like? the interviews? the hopes and dreams? the disappointments? the news "You're hired"? Did you have to relocate? What was that like? What do you remember about the house? Are you in the same house? What memories is the house storing for you?

Savor the memories.

How did you get along with each other's family? Was it the two of you against the in-laws in those prehistoric days? Did you politely accept their advice and then proceed to ignore it? Were the in-laws your good friends, offering advice and support without mingling in your private lives?

Remember how you supported each other: going to night

school, finding a job, fixing up the house or apartment. Whatever it was, you were a team! Wife and husband!

Remember your journeys of faith. Perhaps you joined the Church in the days when the priest personally instructed you in the ABC's of Catholicism. Perhaps you joined the Church through the new-but-ancient process called the RCIA (Rite of Christian Initiation of Adults). Perhaps you were both Catholic; perhaps only one of you is Catholic.

What faith traditions do you each remember from childhood? Are they important and meaningful to you today? Are there some that you would like to integrate into your life today? How can they be modified to respect both traditions?

Whatever your faith journeys have been, entering into marriage has destined the two of you to share that part of your lives. Sharing your faith will open new horizons of understanding for both of you.

Remember the intimacy. Remember how you used to talk for hours. Remember how you longed to be physically close. Remember how time alone was important to you. Remember how comfortable you were sharing your deepest fears and craziest dreams.

Years follow years, and couples easily forget what that kind of friendship was like. Yet, that friendship was — and is — a significant part of the essence of your love for each other. Talk about what that was like. Ask yourselves, "Would we like to recapture some of that vitality? How can we do that?"

The Art of Forgiveness

Grace once given is not taken back. The Spirit that ignited your love for each other years ago remains a part of your relationship today. Be aware of that. Church weddings are normative, but truly Christian marriages are exceptional; those are the marriages that embrace the grace of the Spirit.

Marriages don't need grand-slam infidelities to fizzle and die. It's the little betrayals that in time take their toll: slight discourtesies, moments of defensiveness, and a pattern of failure to prioritize the relationship. These are the betrayals that leave you both wounded and confused.

If you are like most couples who seek marriage counseling, you need to develop the art of forgiveness. When did you last face each other with genuine humility and contrition and admit that you were wrong or thoughtless? How did you apologize in your early years? Did you offer a token of love? a rose? a card? a love letter? Did you admit that a compromise was possible? Did you brainstorm for solutions that you both could respect? What brought about resolution and healing?

Those times of apologizing and reconciling took skill, a skill that came quickly and naturally to the two of you years ago. You still have that capability, you know; you simply have to concentrate more today. Life is packed with kids, jobs, household responsibilities, and social activities, so you have to work a lot harder to exercise the skill that came easily years ago — when life wasn't so "full."

Is the Nest Empty?

"It's just you and me, baby," or so the song goes. Just as the sages predicted, the kids did fly the coop, the endless chauffeuring of them ceased, and there you are, face to face with your spouse. Maybe illness, financial pressures, adjusting to the kids' absence, and the distractions of the aging process have so preoccupied you in recent years that you've forgotten how to successfully negotiate the "empty-nest syndrome."

The empty nest doesn't have to be a jolt. Pull out the scrapbook and photo albums and remember. I'm not suggesting that you idealize a former time; just look for the solutions you may find buried in the treasure chest of your shared memories. Marriages grow stale because couples eat stale bread.

A little success, recaptured and replanted, will move mountains. I've seen this approach work time and time again. As you recall your courtship, your wedding day, your vows, your joys and sorrows, and countless other things, you will discover a gold mine of successes. What worked then can work now. Draw up a list of exceptions; you'll find that you have enough material to write a book yourself.

What? No Memories?

It isn't unusual for couples to say that they can't remember the incidents of years ago. Their lives have been so burdened with distractions, boredom, escape, and responsibilities that they can only recall recent history — where there is very little sweetness to grasp.

Then it is time for the two of you to pull a miracle out of the hat! No, I'm not talking about something supernatural, where the laws of nature are suspended. I pose the miracle to the couple in the following fashion: "When you have your 'miracle,' how will things be different between the two of you?" In fact, I often get even more specific: "How will you act differently when things become the way you'd like them to be?"

Amazingly, the wheels begin to turn, and I am often deluged by practical, feasible steps toward the resolution of marital conflict, resolutions "discovered" by the couple themselves.

Ed and Penny came for counseling. They were stressed to the limit. Ed had no time for Penny; Penny had no time for herself, with three small kids hanging onto her waist. What little time Penny and Ed could salvage at the end of the day was hardly the kind of quality time their marriage needed.

They were not in a mood for make-believe and felt certain that the "remembering" approach was a silly waste of time. Yet, nothing else had worked, so they finally agreed to give it a try.

They closed their eyes and took ahold of their miracle.

"When I have my miracle," Ed mused, "we'll have one meal together without distraction. She'll put down her magazine, and I'll ditch the sports page.

"It will be...let me see...breakfast. I'll get up an hour early, shower, and look like a human being for a change. I'll arrange Friday lunch dates with Penny — just Penny, no kids, every Friday. After eight o'clock each night, Penny and I will talk about us for an hour. No TV!"

Then it was Penny's turn.

"I can see myself getting out of the house an hour a day for aerobics or coffee with a girlfriend. Maybe even a part-time job after I find a reliable baby-sitter. And I need to affirm and support Ed much more than I do."

Within a short time, this couple had generated their own solutions. They cared enough about each other to be honest with their needs. They freed themselves from the rut of the here-and-now by imagining and imaging a future of their own design — not a future based on winning the lottery or rising to the top of the corporate ladder. Rather, they imagined that which was simple — and possible.

The job of the counselor is to support the couple as they make their own miracle happen. As behaviors change, attitudes change, which means feelings change. A change in any of these three ways of relating will shift the marriage toward healing and growth.

Remember the exceptions and miracles and put them to work for your marriage.

 What now is has already been; what is to be, already is; and God restores what would otherwise be displaced.

Ecclesiastes 3:15

∞ GOOD WAYS
TO FIGHT

Anger is a natural emotion in marriage. When two persons share every facet of life, some tension is inevitable.

But how can fighting in marriage be considered a marriage maker? Most couples would insist that their fighting tends to fall into the marriage breakers category. Perhaps they need to make a few simple changes in their fighting patterns.

Couples are often skeptical when they hear that. It's hard to believe that a little change can mean a great deal of change in a positive direction. This simple axiom holds true in the midst of strong tension as well.

If a couple wants to fight (no physical abuse is ever sanctioned!), the counselor will not serve as a referee; however, he or she may offer some creative ways to make the fight a "good" one. When a couple comes to me for marriage counseling, I suggest they try a new twist. In this chapter, I propose nine ways to de-escalate, perhaps even savor, a marital feud.

⊘ WORKING TOGETHER

The following suggestions may sound simplistic, but they're not; they're merely simple. These strategies require your love *for* and commitment *to* each other — nothing more and nothing less.

Change the location of the fight. James and Maria found conflict a delicious pastime. However, their children suffered from nervous disorders and exacerbated asthmatic conditions as a result of the constant outbursts between their parents.

This couple loved each other and their children enough to seek help. First, they pursued lengthy and costly psycho-analysis. Despite the insights they gained, the situation did not improve.

Next, they went to a therapist who suggested they pound pillows and rubber duckies to release their pent-up anger. The result: a couple of good pillow fights and a fetish for rubber duckies.

They next approached the "paid-listener" type of counselor who would respond, "Aha, hum, that's interesting. How do you feel when your screams shatter glass?" With this hands-off approach, James and Maria only felt energized to keep their war going.

Without denying the value of these other techniques, I prefer something a little more novel. When the couple finally came to see me, I suggested that they argue as usual but change the location of the arguing.

Obviously, James and Maria were highly motivated to keep working at this issue; they were very much aware of how their fighting affected the children. The suggestion to change locations for their tense exchanges, however, seemed a bit silly. Nevertheless, they cooperated with the homework assignment.

"Where do you fight?"

"Always in the living room."

"Have you tried fighting in the bathroom?"

"Are you kidding?"

"Not at all. For one week, permit yourself to go ahead with your usual tiffs, but always — always — go to the bathroom to carry them out."

Simple? Yes, and it worked. Don't ask why. Maybe something about the atmosphere in their living room helped provoke or sustain their skirmishes. Perhaps some painful memory was associated with that room. Just carrying on the war in a different setting disoriented them so much that their fights reduced in frequency and intensity. They wanted results, and they got results.

Change the frequency of your fighting. Patty and Mark picked at each other; no full-blown confrontation, just potshots five or six times a day. They would criticize each other's choice of words, opinions, attitudes, or attire. Unlike James and Maria, who enjoyed their fights, Patty and Mark suffered a great deal. The hostility between them was slow, predictable torture. Much of their energy was sapped from the relationship to fuel this barrage; very few pleasant exchanges took place. If only they could call a truce.

With the help of counseling, they did.

Patty and Mark decided to fight good and long. They would take all the time they needed to wrestle with the issue of the moment — *except* on Tuesdays and Fridays. On Tuesdays and Fridays, they would give the battles a rest. They could make love, bake cookies, read alone, take a walk (alone or together), or seek additional counseling, but they could not fight. They had the liberty to resume the fighting on Saturday mornings and Wednesday mornings; but those two days had to be treated like quiet, sacred space.

It worked. By taking the routine out of their hostilities, quality time was allowed to happen. The marriage slowly but surely began to heal.

Change the timing of the fights. Perhaps you can spring out of bed at the crack of dawn, singing the score from "The Sound of Music," while your spouse can write poetry at the stroke of midnight, while dancing the night away. If the two of you operate on a different energy clock, adjusting *when* you fight can diminish the damage to your relationship. The awful things couples say to one another often lose their sting when the timing is different.

Make the dinner hour off-limits for feuding; many couples cannot fight fair after an exhausting day at work or on an empty stomach. Also, postpone an altercation for some time following an especially tense period — only when the in-laws are at least two-days away after "enjoying" a week-long vacation as your guests, for example.

One couple knew they were less defensive late at night; they knew they could be more honest and less hostile if they would just wait until the end of the day to address their issues. Another couple, however, could not adopt that timing because their fatigue caused them to be less caring and more hurtful with each other. Instead, they chose to air their grievances right after the first cup of coffee in the morning. Clearing the air got the day off to a promising start.

Change your timing, and you may change your fighting for the better. It's worth a try.

Change the duration of the fights. Here is some good news for you worriers: it is possible to reserve a specific time of day for your heated exchanges and limit it to, say, a half-hour. It's amazing how quickly you can get to the point when you agree on a time limit. Set an alarm clock; let it tick away the minutes of the fight. When the alarm sounds, it will jolt you back into the other realities of life.

Most sensible couples who enjoy a good argument know there is only so much time in the day to do all the many other things that matter. Why chop up your day into fifty small battles — which is really ongoing civil war — when one designated half hour, hour, or whatever time you agree upon, will do far less damage?

Impossible? Try it.

Add something new to your fights. The Smiths lived dangerously. She had a pilot's license; he was a skydiver. They raced cars together in the summer and skied in the winter.

Yet, when it came to their style of marital discord, they played it dull and safe. They merely screamed at each other from across the room. How average and boring!

I suggested they add a little class to their chaos. "How about yelling at each other in the nude?"

"Preposterous!" they exclaimed together. Yet, the suggestion held a kind of fascination for them — and they tried it. As you might guess, negative passion turned into positive passion. For a couple who dearly loved a thrill a minute, it sure beat their boring shouting matches.

Change the sequence of your daily routine. Take a thorough look at the patterns in your disputes. In charting out their day, one highly stressed couple discovered a certain order to things: at the end of the workday, he would slam through the front door, the kids would scream, she would run to him with a grocery list of complaints, and he would proceed to assume his couch-potato position with the TV blasting. This was daily fare.

In counseling, the couple devised a whole new sequence. When he came home, he would enter the house through the kitchen door and pour coffee for himself and his wife. He would take the coffee to the living room and quietly wait for his wife to join him. With the setting neutralized, the couple could then air the day's shortcomings and pinpoint the good parts of the day with calm and objectivity.

This small, seemingly insignificant arrangement worked wonders. The couple reorganized their routine into a new, positive habit, and the intensity of their fighting abated.

Aim low and be concrete in your expectations. You want peace of mind, happiness, and fulfillment? Lower your standards and be specific.

Unfortunately, the Church has contributed to the fuzziness of our language by talking about such things as global justice and unconditional love. These things are huge and distant and illusive to those of us who prod along day after day just trying to maintain sanity and order in our lives.

We human beings simply cannot grasp such monumental ideals. But we can be conscientious on a smaller scale; we can be courteous, affirming, grateful, and patient. A spouse may feel "justly treated" when her fastidious efforts to wash and wax the car are recognized or "unconditionally loved" when his sinus headache is nursed with tender loving care. These are the seeds for peace of mind, happiness, and fulfillment.

Why do we call ourselves to holiness by way of unattainable goals? We all tend to forget that holiness seldom consists of doing great things, but in doing little things with great love.

Create win-win outcomes. In the playing field of married life, couples can expect one of three outcomes: win-lose, lose-lose, or win-win. They, themselves, can determine the outcome.

Late in the spring, Stan and Irene purchased a home. Stan wanted to paint their new house before the sweltering summer heat hit full force. Irene, suffering from too much winter and a bad case of cabin fever, needed time on the beach. Not that she wasn't excited about their newly purchased home; she just didn't feel the same urgency that Stan felt.

Stan declared that all vacations were off and lambasted his wife for her impracticality. Irene grudgingly gave in. Stan won; Irene lost. End of round one.

After talking with an assertive girlfriend, Irene decided to enter the ring with some new jabs and punches. She approached Stan with a long list of paybacks and took some cheap shots in an effort to entice him to play beach-blanket bingo.

But Stan adamantly refused to budge. He flexed his verbal muscles and clamored that Scripture says man is head of the house. Round two was clearly a lose-lose situation.

In counseling, Irene and Stan put away their boxing gloves and asked each other for a rematch. They were determined to create a win-win outcome.

Stan suggested that Irene help him with the painting for a few hours each evening. Since Irene took pride in their home and recognized the need to maintain it, she was pleased to join Stan in his efforts to finish the painting.

But Irene continued to ask that the weekend be beach time. Stan agreed — and they had more fun than they'd had in a long time.

Because success breeds success, Stan and Irene became masters at the game of win-win. So can you. With patience and determination, you can too.

Wait a week before making drastic decisions. Sometimes fools do rush in where angels fear to tread. Divorce is serious business. In a Church that believes in the permanence of the wedding vows, we are not coming up smelling like roses. Please, someone, somehow, put on the brakes. Just wait a week!

Give yourselves time to cool off, to talk it out, to do something differently, to apply one of these strategies, to rethink. You'll be glad you let time be your friend.

Reward Yourselves

To reinforce the modifications you choose to make your fighting "good," you may want to add a negative consequence or a positive reward. For example, Connie and Jeff decided to implement several of the suggestions above. They agreed that they would take on a messy household chore if they failed to realize some advance toward "good" fighting. On the other hand, they would reward themselves at the end of the month with a fancy meal if their major fights had turned into calm discussions.

Positive or negative reinforcers are excellent tools to help you carve out new marital behaviors.

An Exception

As you can see, these strategies are, indeed, simple. They are offered on the assumption that the two of you are committed to the experience of marriage as a covenant. They assume that the issues in your marriage, although troublesome, burdensome, and frustrating, are nonetheless manageable.

Abuse, however, is something else. If your relationship exists in an environment of compulsive behavior or physical or emotional abuse, these strategies will make little difference. You need the direct input of professionals. This and other good reading material can be helpful, but only the direction of a professional and the community of a support group will bring about the healing that is needed.

In the house of the just there are ample resources.... / A glad heart lights up the face.... / a word in season, how good it is!... / A cheerful glance brings joy to the heart; / good news invigorates the bones.

Proverbs 15:6, 13, 23, 30

∞ HUMOR, PLAY, AND RITUAL

The human being has a creative and playful side, a side most of us don't get in touch with very often. Yet, playfulness and humor have a powerful healing capacity — particularly when couched in little "rituals" that reflect honesty and acceptance. Watching a couple concoct their own remedies, on their own turf, using humor, play, and ritual is a fascinating study.

Most of us can recall small childhood rituals — little gimmicks, facial expressions, hand gestures, or comic one-liners — that conveyed something to or about a sibling. It wasn't meant to hurt — and didn't hurt. Rather, it built a sense of "we're family, and we know one another better than anyone knows us." It engendered a familial intimacy that bonded. When the kids come together years later as adults, these little rituals are recalled in family stories that begin with "remember how" and "remember when."

⊘ WORKING TOGETHER

One of the most interesting forms of building intimacy and maintaining the sweet goodness in a marriage is to ritualize humor and play. Too many couples take themselves too seriously.

Put humor to work for you. Some couples really know how to tease, the kind of teasing that produces good results. I call these friendly duels "love pokes." There are as many different kinds of "love pokes" as there are marriages.

Behind every love poke there is a touch of truth, a truth that would be difficult to convey in a straightforward manner. You catch more flies with honey than with vinegar; in the same way, this approach can be extremely successful. It opens the heart to "hear" because the air is filled with intimate laughter. Much marital anger and arguing are mellowed by this kind of sweet intimacy.

Play with the old "I'm-gonna-tell" technique. Once again, remember your childhood; remember how that line seemed to hold some kind of illusive power? I used to think that one "Ummmm...I'm gonna tell" would so utterly disturb my rival that once the weighty threat was leveled, I could command the person's behavior to suit my own whims.

For adults, of course, the line rings foolish — almost absurd. After all, who are we going to tell? Yet, many couples I've counseled have recounted their fun with this one little caveat. Once one of them realizes that good communication skills or good fighting techniques are not being employed, a playful threat to tell the counselor ("Ummmm...I'm gonna tell") breaks them both into realms of laughter.

There's wisdom here. When a couple begins the counseling process and is given some of the homework mentioned in previous chapters, they develop a certain childlike desire to please the counselor with their results. This isn't unusual, and it isn't unhealthy. The affirming direction of the counselor plays a role in the process; why not have a little fun with it.

Let healthy competition enrich your relationship. It isn't necessary for the two of you to be equal all the time in all things. In fact, you already know you're not. One of you knows more about some things than the other. One of you is better at some things than the other. With this natural difference, playful competition can add a spark of life to your intimacy.

A fact of life which many couples fail to realize is that if one partner changes in any way, the relationship automatically is changed. When someone changes, the intimacy they share with another will have to shift with respect to the change. If one of you excels in some way, the other's best response is to encourage and support the spouse that excels — or, better yet, attempt to foster an interest in the field as well. Especially if sports are involved; a little healthy competition on the tennis court will do wonders for intimacy in the bedroom.

Sadly, many faith-filled married persons often accept an empty, stagnant marital relationship because they are not willing to put the energy into something that is mutually exciting. How refreshing to hear couples challenge each other with heartwarming invitations like "When are you going to join me in exercise class?" or "You don't know what you're missing by not coming to Bible study with me."

When one of you knows a great deal about something or is

especially good at something, the situation is laden with opportunities for resentment, pride, and one-upmanship. But it is also ripe with opportunities to strengthen your marriage.

Build surprise into your marriage. Plan a surprise week. Alternate weeks ("I surprise you this week; you surprise me next week") or set aside one week a month when you surprise each other as often as you like. This game creates a sense of expectancy and spices up a dull relationship. You're kept on your toes to think of things to do — and you're kept on your toes anticipating the surprise of your lover.

Gayle and Roger filled their hours and days with worry. They even worried about having nothing to worry about. They expected the worst, and usually got it. When they looked back at yesterday, they were filled with regret; when they looked ahead to tomorrow, they were filled with dread.

The intervention of creating surprises brought joy back into their marriage. One week, Gayle surprised Roger with a steak and champagne dinner. When it was his turn to do the surprising, Roger composed a love poem for Gayle and left it on her pillow before going to work.

Over time, their gloom-and-doom approach to life started to fade. They didn't become silly about life's real problems, but they experienced much less stress. A little fun lifted their heavy outlook on life; they were able to handle problems more effectively.

Build surprise into your marriage; see what happens.

Take ten minutes to do the this-is-my-life exercise. Lock yourselves in a quiet room — no phones or interruptions of any kind — and take five minutes each to talk only about yourself: your day, your mood, how you're feeling physically, whatever. While one is talking, the other listens attentively, without comment or question. This is not a problem-solving session; it is strictly a time for self-disclosure.

Caught up in the rat race, you may seldom get in touch with your own feelings or know what those feelings are. How, then, can you give to your life partner that which you don't even allow yourself to own?

Couples often report that the faithful practice of this ten-minute exercise increases self-acceptance, self-awareness, other-acceptance, and other-awareness — which is what healthy intimacy is all about.

You don't need a baby-sitter, you don't need to spend money, you don't need to carve a great deal of time out of your day. It's so easy; try it.

Celebrate your mistakes. When results aren't quick enough, couples often get discouraged. Once you've set out to implement some of these marriage makers, keep your expectations reasonable. If you find yourself falling short of your goals and slipping back into old patterns, take advantage of the rich harvest of information that becomes available to you in the moments commonly considered "failures."

Ben made two firm resolutions: he would not run home to Mom everytime he had a squabble with his wife, Donna, and he would reduce the time he spent watching television.

For three months, Ben prided himself on keeping his resolutions. He and Donna were growing closer, and they both knew that the exercise of his resolutions was a main factor. But when Ben fell from grace on both resolves, the couple plunged into depression.

This couple found it difficult to believe that every negative contains a positive potential for learning about oneself. But when Ben applied this principle, he saw the chain of cause-and-effect.

His mother had always made excuses for him and never asked what part he played in conflicts at school or at work. Donna, on the other hand, gently but directly confronted Ben about his abrasive manner with others. The television was a way to block out any feedback that would make him grow up.

Analyzing that slip-up, negative as it felt, Ben realized the extent to which he depended — in an unhealthy way — on his mother's affirmation and coddling. He was able to pinpoint the television as a means of escape to avoid conflict.

This took great courage and energy on Ben's part. He had to be willing to strip away pride, fear, and defensiveness to get to that deeper layer of immaturity. Because Ben and Donna started with a positive approach and used the mistakes, regressions, and slip-ups as life-generating opportunities, they seldom stayed in a rut for long.

Develop your own forgiveness rituals. Forgiveness is a rich part of our Catholic tradition in which the two of you can tap. There are formal and community ways of celebrating forgiveness and reconciliation, and there are informal and personal ways to celebrate this kind of healing.

The communal form of reconciliation, with Scripture readings, an examination of conscience, and a homily all focused on sins against marriage, is a key ritual that would be invaluable to the two of you. Encourage your parish to celebrate this sacrament with this unique theme at least once a year. The service highlights sins of omission, since what couples *do not do* for one another cries to be addressed and called by name.

You can also build your own personalized reconciliation service into your daily routine. Phil and Linda "confess" to each other just before bedtime every night. They may take a verse from Scripture such as "I came that they may have life" and admit there were times during the day when they were not life-giving toward each other. The old silent treatment, biting remarks, and simply ignoring each other's needs are ways that life is choked out of a marriage rather than channeled into it.

This couple also designed a kind of "absolution" that they pray over each other. The ritual is a sacramental that has great healing power for the two of them.

Play with your talents. A seemingly unrelated strength from another sphere of your life can be called upon to bolster your marriage.

The Greens had suffered one frustration after another: costly illnesses, bothersome in-laws, and children who flirted with breaking the law. Their setbacks and major disappointments threatened to overwhelm them — but they pulled through. They played on talents from their past.

They had both grown up on farms and could recall many desperate situations in which sheer stubbornness had pulled their families through crises. They borrowed that quality of stubbornness from their childhood and put it into play in their married life to steady them through hardships and disappointments.

Mike borrowed from his work life to improve his marriage and family life. For many years, Mike suffered from severe headaches and a growing sense of personal failure. He and his wife were expecting their third child. Mike had a social-work background and had connected with industry as a consultant for troubled employees.

Mike was good at what he did. He carefully and patiently listened to his clients as they described high levels of stress in their lives. He discussed ways to break down overwhelming projects into small, manageable tasks. He eventually became very skilled at this approach.

At home, however, Mike felt overwhelmed. He battled his

headaches constantly and felt that what little time he had for his wife and children was far from quality.

When Mike reviewed some of the areas of his life where he felt less overwhelmed, he thought of his work. He pinpointed the skills he used there and thought about ways he could put those skills into play at home to enhance relationships and gain some peace of mind.

Mike decided to play self-counselor, counseling himself the way he would counsel the people he worked with. He told himself to divide his time into small units instead of mammoth projects and to develop some time-management discipline.

Each evening, Mike would devote a half-hour to each child. They may play a game, watch TV, or tackle homework problems. It wasn't what they did but the fact that father and child — together — were focused on one thing.

Mike paced himself through the evening, however, to reserve energy for meaningful time with his wife after the children were in bed. They would talk, read, watch a video, or go to bed early. Mike's headaches vanished, and so did his sense of failure. Playing on a strength from another sector of his life brought renewal and fresh meaning to life.

Mary did the same thing. She loved to arrange flowers. Her clientele enjoyed her lighthearted nature and the sweet, warm atmosphere of her floral shop. She made her little place of business an environment that renewed and refreshed. Not so, her home and marriage.

There, the weeds grew tall and wild, with sunny days few and far between. The house was always a mess, meals were dull, and her personal appearance was usually less than glamorous.

It hit Mary one day in my office: "If my home and marriage could match the shop!" With further thought, she envisioned some changes that would make that very thing possible. With a few floral arrangements, Mary added a fresh look to several rooms in her home, a look that tends to make one automatically feel better about the environment. She organized household chores and began to take greater pride in her appearance. Her husband fell in love with her all over again.

You Two Are the Experts

These games and rituals can enhance and enrich the quality of your marriage. Some of them will be more effective for your relationship than others.

But you two are the experts. No one knows your relationship like you know it. You know your own limitations, inhibitions, likes, and dislikes. You know the areas that cause you the most difficulty and you know the areas that bring the most satisfaction.

As you embrace your covenant with fidelity, the Holy Spirit will lead and direct you. You can invent your own games and rituals or adapt these to suit your needs. Great peace, healing, and wholeness is your inheritance.

 You changed my mourning into dancing; / you took off my sackcloth and clothed me with galdness...

Psalm 30:12

◯◯ MARRIAGE AND THE TEN COMMANDMENTS

Healthy spirituality plays an enormous part in the shaping and saving of marriages. Many couples never seem to understand or accept the grace of the sacrament. Those that do, manifest the presence of Christ in their relationship with each other, in the relationships they have with their children, and in the way they relate with others.

The Ten Commandments (see Deuteronomy 5:7-21) embody rich insights for those couples who choose to live a sacramental marriage.

You shall not have other gods besides me. Our society is movie-oriented. Does our culture invent the ideas we see in the movies or merely reflect them? For instance, young people leaving the theater after viewing the megahit *Ghost* were fighting back tears and exclaiming things like "It was awesome!"

Yet, what they were in awe of was a dead man who in life was afraid to commit himself to the woman he lived with, afraid to say "I'll love you forever," afraid of marriage. The audience idolized the false god of romantic commitment, which is likely to be no commitment at all. Movies about happily married couples doing the ordinary chores associated with married life don't tend to be box-office hits.

The false gods of workaholism, alcoholism, materialism, and secularism demand human sacrifices. Time and energy spent worshiping these gods rob quality time and energy from your marriage. These dangerous deities can push your real feelings out of the way as they goad you on in hot pursuit of other things.

Too much faith placed in the authority of Oprah Winfrey, Donahue, and Geraldo have replaced trust in God's Word about what makes marriages succeed. Sometimes television parades bizarre liaisons as role models of marriages of the future.

If your marriage is a sacrament, you will reject these false gods. The living and true God speaks of married love as stable, permanent, and faithful. Any other kind of love is an illusion that cannot and will not sustain a lasting marriage.

You shall not take the name of the Lord, your God, in vain. This commandment means much more than simply refraining from saying "bad words." It means acknowledging God as the third Partner in your marriage — and living that reality in concrete ways. Do you bless each other in God's name? Do you heal each other in God's name? Do you intercede for each other? Are you able to speak intimately with each other about your personal walk with God? Are you able to speak intimately together *to* God? Do you undertake projects together in the name of the Lord, especially by helping others and serving the poor?

Just to know that you can call upon the name of God is a comfort. To exercise that privilege is a priceless gift of grace. How do the two of you consciously welcome God into your marriage?

Take care to keep holy the Sabbath day. Married couples who keep Sunday special are very wise, indeed. What sounds like a restriction is really a tremendous freedom for couples.

Six days a week of work, hectic schedules, chauffeuring, and a million other activities merit some time out. Go for a walk, have coffee with other married couples, read old love letters, pray together, play games, visit: all these are holy endeavors that honor the Sabbath.

If you have children, you have to guard your sacred time together. You need to convey to the children that the two of you need and want time for yourselves, if only for an hour on Sunday afternoon or evening. Children will grow to appreciate and respect this rule on the Sabbath. Hopefully, they will apply it to their own marriages one day.

How lonely it is for one spouse and the children to worship on the Sabbath while the other spouse is absent for some reason. The parish is meant to be more than just a spiritual truck stop where you pull in for a quick fill-up. It is a place of refreshment and renewal.

Many parishes now sponsor Marriage Encounter weekends or romantic evenings of reflection for married couples (baby-sitting provided). Give this book as a gift to your pastor. Maybe it will generate some new ideas and creative approaches to ministering to married couples in your parish.

Honor your father and your mother. Many married couples have unfinished business with their parents. Old mental tapes that were uncritically absorbed tend to be instantly replayed at the strangest times. For better or worse, your parents' attitudes have fashioned your attitudes toward intimacy, affection, sexuality, communication, commitment, and other critical areas of life.

Do you see yourself reacting to squabbles in self-defeating ways? Do you have unrealistic expectations about your mate and wonder where such ideas come from? Are you repeating the same mistakes your parents made in their marriages, even though you promised yourself you wouldn't?

Honoring your parents may mean coming to terms with their foibles and inadequacies, rejecting the faulty notions and attitudes that they passed on to you, and ultimately, forgiving them for hurting you.

This is not to suggest that certain grave issues can be addressed with simplistic solutions or naive approaches. If you were abused in any way by your parents, you deserve the best professional treatment you can get. Now!

This book is speaking primarily to couples who have come from loving but imperfect and perhaps dysfunctional homes. There may be a real need for reality-testing, reconciliation, and some demonstrated appreciation and affection directed toward your parents in spite of their failures.

As you take care of unfinished business with your parents, you find that you also begin to address unfinished business in your marriage. Healing individuals constitute healing marriages.

You shall not kill. Perhaps you don't actually slug it out with your spouse. But in marriage, one can kill more than the body. Marital intimacy is the ultimate intimacy, short of our life with

God. You become consummately vulnerable. You know how to hurt each other. Because of this, you can kill each other's spirit with little effort.

Marital discord is often pockmarked with the scars of many little jabs and insensitivities. A forgotten birthday, a betrayal of a confidence, insensitive remarks: all of these add up. After years of enduring such jabs, the relationship is in grave peril.

Many a marriage dies of malnutrition. When was the last time the two of you attended a lecture on marriage, went on a retreat together, read a book that enriched your intimacy? Ask yourselves, "What can we do that serves as nourishment for our relationship to keep it alive?"

You shall not commit adultery. Infidelity is connected to "You shall not kill." Adultery is a mortal sin, not because it involves sex but because it deals a deathblow to individuals and relationships. Becoming intimately involved with someone other than your life partner and soul mate is the ultimate dishonesty; it turns into a cancer that quietly (or perhaps not so quietly) eats away at the core of your marriage.

Marital fidelity means much more than not having intercourse with a person other than your spouse. It also means the hard work of creating an environment between the two of you that includes certain exclusive dimensions. If you're not working at deepening your love or if you share more with a friend than you do with your spouse, you are indeed being unfaithful.

You shall not steal. So you don't dip into each other's billfolds or steal from the joint savings account. But there are other ways to "steal" from each other. For example, do you diminish each other's individuality?

In most marriages there are times when one spouse sacrifices for the benefit of the other (postponing future education or working a second job, for example), but to squelch your partner's talents or suppress his or her personality and unique gifts are sins against this commandment.

In the marriage covenant, you are cheerleaders for each other. Right now, put down this book and ask each other, "How can I help you become more of who you want to become?"

You shall not bear dishonest witness against your neighbor. Your neighbor is not only the refugee in the Middle East or the bag lady in the inner city or the people next door. Your neighbor is also the person snoring right next to you in bed. Go ahead; take a good look at that person. That's the one you are supposed to love as yourself. It can be much easier to love the stranger in the Middle East, the poor lady on the street corner downtown, or the crabby people next door than your overweight mate who has bad breath in the morning.

When you make fun of your spouse or disclose certain intimacies that no one else has the right to know, you bear dishonest witness against your neighbor: your spouse. In-law triangles often form as a result of this kind of dishonest witnessing. He tells Mom, "She isn't and never will be the cook you are." She tells Dad, "He isn't manly; he isn't a take-charge kind of guy."

Face your nearest neighbor — your spouse — and work things out.

You shall not covet your neighbor's wife. The wording of this commandment is not inclusive; it covers both genders and reminds you that the grass is not greener on the other side. No matches are made in heaven, but there are plenty of comfortable compromises made here on earth.

The lovely, submissive wife on the *Donna Reed Show* of yesteryear and the man's man on *Father Knows Best* never existed. Neither does the idyllic couple on *Little House on the Prairie.*

Fantasize all you want in the bedroom, but in the daylight hours, what you see is what you get. A loving outlook recognizes that your beloved is not perfect by cultural standards — but he or she is, indeed, perfect for you.

You shall not covet anything that belongs to your neighbor. Married couples often complain about reckless spending and financial appetites that are too big for the pocketbook. Why, then, do couples reminisce about the good old days when life was simpler and money scarcer?

Why do couples frequently list "fights over money" as a major reason for breaking up? The simple life and simple pleasures are the things that really last; this is Christ's message. Do you believe he was right? Besides the simple intimacy, honesty, and fidelity you share, what greater treasure could you possibly desire? Remember Jesus' words: "For where your treasure is, there also will be your heart" (Luke 12:34).

Your Personal Belief System

Looking at laws or commandments as "don't this" and "don't that" can leave you feeling chained, restricted, and inhibited. Unfortunately, this is a common interpretation of the Ten Commandments.

If you turn the Ten Commandments into a personal belief system, however, you end up with a positive orientation. The commandments can become a loving code to live by when you claim them as a marital creed.

We place our faith in God.
We let God be our intimate "third Partner."
We take time for ourselves.
We become healthy today by healing our pasts.
We do things that nourish our relationship.
We give our deepest selves only to each other.
We support and encourage each other.
We respect each other at all times.
We extend unconditional acceptance to each other.
We keep life simple.

What a rich path for the two of you to follow as lovers and life partners!

 The promises of the LORD are sure, / like tried silver, freed from dross, sevenfold refined. / You, O LORD, will keep us / and preserve us always.
Psalm 12:7-8

⚭ MARRIAGE
AND THE BEATITUDES

Jesus gave us a riddle: lose yourself and you will find yourself. As much as I would like to give marriage workshops and retreats all over the country, as much as I would like for you to read marriage-enrichment material, I cannot make you or your marriage happy.

Christ said that happiness is the by-product of a certain way of living. The truth is that if you follow all the directives in this book, you will improve your marriage, but you still will not be happy until you place your marriage at the service of others.

Although the Sermon on the Mount has been traditionally interpreted as a timeless message for individual disciples, surely there were married people in that teachable crowd who took the beatitudes home with them. Indeed, they do apply to marriage.

Happy are the poor in Spirit; theirs is the kingdom of heaven. Scripture tells us that the poor have a special place in the heart of God. All those who opened their hearts to Jesus were in some way poor: they had very little, they knew they were sinners, they were childlike in their approach to God. All these persons, although classified as "poor," found happiness and riches in Jesus Christ.

Is it quantity or quality that makes you happy? In terms of material comfort, what and how much do you need to be happy? How many cars do you really *need?* How big a house is *big enough?* How much financial security is *responsible?*

Many couples tithe a good portion of their income to the needy; others give not only their money but also their time and their love. One young couple donates an hour a week at a shelter for the homeless, serving soup and doing dishes. Another couple takes a nursing-home resident to dinner once a month. These Christian couples see their resources — money, time, and talent — as treasures to be shared. They know when enough is enough, and they are happy. They know that their resources, none of them, are truly theirs.

Sinners were also the poor whom Jesus made rich. They knew they were weak, vulnerable, and helpless. Yet, because they knew they were weak, vulnerable, and helpless, they knew their strength. In marriage, spiritual poverty is evidenced in several ways.

For example, when you're weak, you ask for help. You seek professional help when your health is endangered; you seek financial guidance with monetary resources. As a Christian couple, you know you cannot travel the way of the world by yourselves. As broken, imperfect persons, you acknowledge your poverty and need for God's grace. This is spiritual poverty.

Spiritual poverty is also manifested in your need for forgiveness — and in your *knowing* you're in need of forgiveness. In the embrace of marital intimacy, "I'm sorry" — as well as "I forgive you" — is crucial. The Lord is very specific about this: he directs all of us to do this "seventy-seven times" (Matthew 18:22).

Finally, you know spiritual poverty in your marriage when you embrace quiet wisdom — and humbly share that wisdom with others. Very likely, the two of you have gained wisdom from many differend forms of pain and joy you've known over the years: a divorce, a new friendship, the death of a loved one, career satisfactions, financial struggles. What happiness there is in sharing that wisdom with an inexperienced couple who needs a mentor and guide.

Childlike persons are poor because they view everything as a gift, opening their hands wide in trust and vulnerability. Be childlike in your love for God and each other. Put away your inhibitions and insecurities and play! Rediscover the wonders of the world.

Happy the gentle; they shall have the earth for their heritage. When you no longer say "thank you" and "please" to each other, when you no longer surprise each other with a cup of coffee, when you stop giving each other a kiss before leaving for work, when you no longer touch with playfulness, marital gentleness is evaporating.

Two persons in love sensitize each other to all that is lovable in life: other persons, nature, animals. When you are in love, you love the world. As you see yourself through your lover's eyes, you laugh gently at your own quirks. The deadly seriousness of the morning newspaper is offset by the tenderness of an arm across your shoulder, a word of encouragement, and a promise to save the best for later in the day.

Jesus is gentle of heart, and he calls his married disciples to that outlook on life. In the sacrament of marriage, you offer your hearts, made gentle by your love for each other, to those who seek rest from overwhelming burdens. The solid bond of your marital friendship makes your loving support something that others are drawn to, something they can trust.

Your sacrament is not just for you; it is also for others. Your happiness and fulfillment rest in the two of you loving each other and the world with open arms rather than arms wrapped tightly around yourselves — blocking yourselves in and the world out. The whole universe is yours, and it hungers for your gentle, healing touch.

Happy are those who mourn; they shall be comforted. This is a kissing cousin to gentleness. The Lord is not recommending a sentimental crying jag for therapeutic reasons. God wants us to see reality through Christ's eyes.

People don't want or need your pity. What they could use is your empathy. Every parish would be wise to offer support groups for couples who share common struggles and concerns. Could you help organize and be part of such a group?

As you know, your relationship passes through stages: infatuation, romance, disillusionment, parenting, the empty nest, retirement, and old age. Each stage demands some kind of grief work. A wise pastoral staff will facilitate this.

Can you imagine how empty your marriage would be if you were preoccupied solely with your own problems? To be oblivious or numb to the pain of others around you can hardly be called "marital bliss."

Be compassionate; mourn for yourselves and mourn for others. Find happiness in bonding with other Christian couples who share your life views. Reach out to help and heal the wounded all around you.

Happy are those who hunger and thirst for what is right; they shall be satisfied. To be too heavenly-minded appears to lack earthly purpose. To be sure, much of what is sacred to marriage is in danger. The media bashes and ridicules the family, tallies the statistics of violence and sexual abuse, and relays the right-to-die drums beating out the dance of "mercy killing." The homeless have become merely an eyesore, addiction comes in any flavor you want, and AIDS is rampant. As married persons, does all this make you angry?

Catholics believe the teaching in the Letter of James: "For just as a body without a spirit is dead, so also faith without works is dead" (2:26). How happy will you be when you lobby, organize, protest, and act for justice. You will never be satisfied merely including these problems in a pious prayer of the faithful during Mass.

The Church — which is you — needs concrete, specific, small-step action right now. As long as you hunger and thirst, there is hope — and a chance for happiness. Get involved and stay involved. Work for what is right — and make a difference, regardless how insignificant it may seem.

Happy the merciful; they shall have mercy shown them. Are you putting your married foot in your mouth every time you pray the Lord's Prayer: "...forgive us our trespasses, as we forgive those who trespass against us..."? These words beg for and extend forgiveness and mercy: no more, no less.

The two of you can show mercy in many practical ways. For example, there are millions of dropout, cop-out, left-out Catholics in our country alone who need to be touched by someone. One could use a visit from you.

We are now on the verge of celebrating two thousand years of Christianity. The pope and bishops are calling for strong Catholic evangelization efforts, even to the point of knocking on doors and visiting homes. How can the two of you respond to this call?

Many couples drift aimlessly and have little purpose in life, yet somehow they survive. Many have been baptized but have had no formation in the Faith. What little faith direction they have received has been picked up from TV preachers and New Age gurus. How can the two of you respond to their needs?

Scan your neighborhood. Can the two of you do some faith-sharing right in your own home? After bowling or a card game, you might very well be in a better position to discuss questions about faith than a priest would be. As a caring married team, the two of you are far less threatening than "Father" and can significantly impact lives.

You may be the ones who inform a nonpracticing Catholic couple that they are not excommunicated just because they were divorced and have remarried. You can help begin the reconciliation process by reaching out with some compassion and mercy to those couples who may feel that Mother Church has put them out on the doorstep and slammed the door.

Finally, there are those alienated by all the changes in the Church. Educate yourselves; learn what the changes of the past twenty-five years have meant. Then share your knowledge authoritatively.

All around you are couples who need and want God's mercy and forgiveness but don't know where to find it. Perhaps the two of you were in that very situation at one time. Happy are you who show mercy. And happy are they who receive it, thanks to you.

Happy the pure of heart; they shall see God. Even the very best marriage knows loneliness at one time or another: the loneliness of separation as well as the ache that arises from the realization that married love, beautiful and fulfilling as it is, does not completely fill the void in your soul. It isn't meant to. Only God can do that.

Time spent in personal, private prayer or on retreats can give the two of you a taste of future joy. Having a spiritual director walk with you on your journey with the Lord will not take anything away from your marriage: in fact, it will enrich you and thereby enrich your spouse.

You are instruments of grace for each other. You cause each other to grow holy by the give-and-take of your relationship. Are you less selfish now because of life shared with your spouse? Have you learned to die to yourself so to enter the death-resurrection plan of Christ himself through the sacrament of marriage? Then truly you are growing in holiness.

The pure of heart see God as their ultimate happiness. A life in union with Christ is the main purpose of living. But married people do not have to look to the extraordinary to find their Lord. The ordinary things of married living — meals shared, chores shared, lovemaking, common pain and joy — make you holy.

The pure of heart will see God at death because God has been no stranger in life. For the pure of heart, eternal happiness starts right now.

Happy the peacemakers; they shall be called sons and daughters of God. Human history is scarred by the violence of war. Governments cross continents to engage in war and countries are torn apart from within their own boundaries as a result of civil conflicts. But you need not tread foreign soil or take sides in civil controversies to find yourselves engaged in war. The most fierce of all warring is often staged at the kitchen table, on the couch, or in the bed.

Because so much hostility can build in marriage, conflict-resolution skills are paramount. No doubt, you've learned the value of strong communication skills as you've attempted to understand each other in countless situations. Peacemaking is so central a value to gospel living that we must do more than pay lip service to it. We must teach it! What can you do to encourage others to learn these same skills? What can your parish do? Sons and daughters of the living God, make peace, not war!

Happy are those persecuted in the cause of right; theirs is the kingdom of heaven. A television evangelist promises prosperity. He even has couples give testimonies about the rewards of religion: a long series of marvelous success stories. God is depicted as a giant spiritual aspirin waiting to be pulled from some heavenly shelf to alleviate life's headaches and to make all things right. In this scenario, the cross is never mentioned. Reputable theologians often refer to this as "cheap grace."

As a Christian couple, you march to a different beat. Your values are not likely to win many votes in our world. "The first shall be last...the greatest among you must serve the rest... love your enemy...die to yourself to live." All these teachings of Christ can really irk people. And when you step on their toes by being out of step, you probably will get nailed. Jesus Christ did, and he predicted it for those who follow him. Read the fine print.

While couples should never seek martyrdom or pain for the sake of pain, a tolerance for a certain amount of persecution and discomfort is wise and spiritually realistic.

While weddings often display slogans like "They tied the knot" or "They bit the dust," Jesus the Lord calls married people to be the light of the world and the salt of the earth.

And if someone complains that your light is too bright and your salt is too tart, you know you're doing good work.

 "Whoever follows me will not walk in darkness, but will have the light of life."

John 8:12

∞ CONCLUSION

To discover the greatest marriage maker of all, ask your-selves, "Exactly what does marriage mean? What is marriage? What does it look like?" Your answer will come from the life you've shared over the years.

Jan and Dick have been married thirty-seven years. Their answer to this question rests against the positives and negatives they've experienced.

"To me," Jan states, "marriage means eight kids and always being in debt because of them; lots of tuna-noodle casseroles and measles and mumps; holding hands with Dick in the bleachers as we watch a million football games, basketball games, and band concerts; minivacations because we couldn't afford the maxi ones. And now it means grandchildren; lots and lots of grandchildren. So our home is still as active and busy as it ever was.

"It also means being proud to wear this ring," Jan holds out her hand, "and waking up each morning knowing that I'm exactly where I'm supposed to be — where I want to be — sharing my life with my husband and loving every moment of it."

Dick looks deeply into Jan's eyes. He speaks in a soft voice. "To me, marriage is having my wife stay by my bedside night and day for two long weeks when it looked like I wouldn't survive the heart attack." Tears fill the eyes of both of them. "It means exactly what the vows say it should mean: 'for better, for worse, for richer, for poorer, in sickness and in health, until death do us part.' " Dick squeezes Jan's hand.

Tracy and Ken have been married for ten years. They have a different understanding of marriage. "Marriage is sharing everything about my life with Ken," admits Tracy. "Ken is my very best friend, someone I trust — second only to God — with all that I have and all that I am. You can't have a marriage without trust. It's impossible."

"And respect is part of that trust," adds Ken. "Tracy goes out of her way to affirm me and make me feel good about myself. She never puts me down or criticizes me unreasonably. I respect what she says because I trust her.

"I try to do the same for her. I like to tell Tracy how beautiful she is, especially her heart. She's so caring and loving toward everyone. I look for creative ways to let her know I admire that in her. Respect is one of the main reasons our relationship has worked so well."

Michelle and Mark are newlyweds; they've been married a year. "I think that the heart of marriage is commitment," insists Michelle, "sticking together through thick and thin, especially during the times when a lot of adjustment is taking place."

Michelle pauses. "There is an awful lot of give-and-take in

a marriage. Sometimes I feel I'm doing all the giving; at other times, I feel like I'm doing all the taking. It really makes you grow up fast. If you don't possess some basic maturity, it just won't work. Even with maturity, it's not easy."

"I really enjoy being married to Michelle," Mark adds. "She makes marriage sound so serious, but I like all the fun we have together — like eating popcorn and watching videos together on Friday nights, then sleeping late on Saturday mornings." He glances at Michelle. "And then making love when you wake up." She blushes and smiles.

Gwen and Todd have been married fourteen years. "I believe marriage is a vocation," Gwen offers, "a special call from God to a special kind of service. And I don't just mean bringing children into the world and forming them into decent human beings." She looks at Todd. "I mean helping each other grow into decent human beings. I would call it the great sacrament of growth that only God's grace makes possible."

Todd nods in agreement. "I also think marriage demands a lot of balancing between independence and interdependence. There are times when Gwen and I are as close as two human beings can possibly be. But there are other times when we give each other plenty of space — and even some distance. It works for us, but it takes plenty of work to make it work."

Four couples, eight varying perspectives on marriage — each just a little different, but none of them wrong. These couples have found within themselves their own marriage makers. With time and trial and error, they have discovered what works and what doesn't work. Their commitment to each other, their entire life experience, their covenanted friendship: these are their own unique marriage makers.

There is no single best description of marriage. In part, this is because marriage is probably the most multifaceted kind of relationship there is. To take two complex persons, often possessing widely differing viewpoints, gifts, and interests, and ask them to blend their lives together in harmony without the loss of their uniqueness and individuality is one of the greatest challenges any human being can face.

In this book, we've profiled many relationships. These couples have relied on the grace of their sacrament to utilize their own unique marriage makers. Some of the marriage makers reviewed here resemble marriage makers you may be familiar with; others may be new to you. We applaud the ingenuity of couples who create and use their own special marriage makers; we applaud those couples who courageously admit that the greatest marriage maker they can exercise is to seek professional marriage counseling when it's needed.

National statistics indicate that one out of two marriages end in divorce in this country; obviously, there are plenty of marriage breakers at work. Yet, marriage breakers need not be fatal. They need to be recognized and neutralized before they wreak their havoc and destruction. Seeking professional help when you need it is a marriage maker only the two of you can exercise.

Your marriage is like fine china; it can chip and break easily. Yet, with gentle care and devotion, your love affair can last a lifetime.

The man and his wife were both naked, yet they felt no shame.
Genesis 2:25

More Helps for Married Couples...

With This Ring
A Practical Guide for Newlyweds
by Renee Bartkowski

Using real-life examples to reinforce her points, the author thoroughly covers the experience of marriage from basic human relating to sexuality to spirituality. Each chapter is followed by a think-and-do section. *$4.50*

Prayers for Married Couples
by Renee Bartkowski

This bestseller contains over 75 brief prayers to help married couples express their hopes, concerns, and dreams. Spouses can use it to build a more spiritual union—with God and with each other. *$3.95*

How to Survive Being Married to a Catholic
A Redemptorist Pastoral Publication

Using a lively cartoon format—along with text—this book gives clear and honest answers to over 80 questions often asked by non-Catholic partners in interfaith marriages. *$4.95*

Order from your local bookstore or write to
Liguori Publications
Box 060, Liguori, MO 63057-9999
*(Please add $1 for postage and handling for
orders under $5; $1.50 for orders over $5.)*